Rebellion
in Río Arriba
1837

Rebellion in Río Arriba 1837

Janet Lecompte

Published in cooperation
with the Historical Society
of New Mexico

University of New Mexico Press
Albuquerque

Library of Congress Cataloging in Publication Data

Lecompte, Janet, 1923–
  Rebellion in Río Arriba, 1837.

  "Published in cooperation with the Historical
Society of New Mexico."
  Includes documents translated from the Spanish.
  Bibliography: p.
  Includes index.
    1. New Mexico—History—To 1848. 2. New Mexico—
History—To 1848—Sources. 3. Mexicans—New Mexico—
History—19th century. 4. Mexicans—New Mexico—History
—19th century—Sources. I. Title.
F800.L43   1985   978.9′03   84-28055
ISBN 0-8263-0800-7
ISBN 0-8263-0801-5 (pbk.)

Design by David R. Margolin

Contents

Illustrations

Foreword

The Historical Society of New Mexico is pleased to cospon-
sor *Rebellion in Río Arriba, 1837* as the seventh title in the
joint publication program between the Society and the University of New Mexico Press. As with the other volumes in
this series, Janet Lecompte's book is on a topic and a period
that heretofore had not received careful historical analysis.

The uprising in northern New Mexico in August 1837
resulted in the death of the governor and sixteen of his
officials. This rebellion was both an armed protest and a fundamental threat to the government, yet until now it has never
been recreated using accounts left by the participants. From
the documents they left, Lecompte unravels for the first time
the complex social and political events surrounding the
uprising.

As a form of protest, rebellions often broke out in the
late eighteenth and early nineteenth century in Spanish
America. These uprisings were early stirrings of what turned
into the independence movement after 1810. But the northern frontier of Mexico remained peaceful during that era of
turbulence in Spain's empire. In New Mexico local conditions were little affected by Mexico's independence for the
first fifteen years of the republic. Then in 1836 Mexico sent
to Santa Fe a new governor, Albino Pérez. Shortly after his
arrival he proclaimed a new constitution, replaced officials,
and announced his intention to collect taxes. The turmoil
that erupted over Pérez's actions is the subject of *Rebellion in
Río Arriba, 1837.*

Preface

The northern province of New Mexico, called Río Arriba, was inhabited mostly by two groups of people—sedentary Pueblo Indians and Spanish-speaking descendants of conquistadors. The latter were among the humblest of human beings. Isolated for over two hundred years from the government of their country, remote from centers of learning or civilization, ignorant of almost all past human endeavor, they were skilled only in hunting, farming, raising sheep and cattle, and fighting nomadic Indians who were sometimes their blood brothers. Their lives were spare and hard, but they had certain freedoms: it was their right, for instance, to choose their own local officials, and to pay no taxes.

In 1835 a new governor, Albino Pérez came to New Mexico from the distant Mexican capital where very few New Mexicans had ever been. He was a sophisticated man with ideas foreign to his constituents. Before long he tried to impose a constitution and laws which the people believed would repeal their freedoms. Wildly angry, the men of Río Arriba, both Hispanic and Indian, rose in a mob against what they saw as oppression, declaring their reasons for revolt in a barely literate statement. Then they murdered the governor and his officers.

In spite of the rebels' bloody waste of talented men, their

democratic principles found support at first among the leaders of the region. To form a new government, the rebels chose from among themselves a governor named José Gonzales, a good, brave man, but ignorant of politics. The new governor could not control the mob that had elected him, nor its several dissenting factions. Soon the factions were spreading terror and anarchy among the people.

Without a leader and a well-expressed goal, without experience in governing, without political acumen in gaining support, the rebels lost control. Powerful men of the territory pooled their superior knowledge and resources. An army under former governor Manuel Armijo seized the government, crushed the leaders, and declared in favor of patriotism and of the Supreme Government, which had neglected them before and would again. And the rebels returned to their farms.

The story of this sad little rebellion has been told many times, but almost always from the viewpoint of the Anglo-Americans, some of whom witnessed it, many of whom wrote about it, and all of whom colored it with their own misunderstandings and bias. The present account is based on primary Mexican sources containing the words and voices of the participants. Here there are no villains and no heroes, no right and no wrong, just an incident of history told by the people involved in it.

All translations are mine unless otherwise noted. In the translations, I have used standard modern accents on names, even though proper names in the original documents lacked them, or added them in an inconsistent fashion. Modern practice insists that we have accents on Abréu and Álvarez, but not on Alarid, which is just the reverse of what New Mexicans would have done in 1837. The name of José Gonzales would be spelled González today, but not in his own time. Then there is the matter of *don* or *Don*, the common title of a gentleman. In the Republican period of New Mexico the word was always capitalized, and often abbreviated to D^n. Today, at least in some circles, the word is not capitalized, and so you will find both versions in this book, depending upon whether the writer of the word is now living or has been dead for a century and a half.

I am indebted to a host of helpers—to David Holtby, Myra Ellen Jenkins, Marc Simmons, and David Weber who read the manuscript and made suggestions; to Carrie Arnold, Donald D. Jackson, Arthur Olivas, Orlando Romero, Richard Rudisill, Richard Salazar, Betty Taylor, Dan Tyler, Luther Wilson, Myron Wood and other friends and scholars who aided me in various ways. For my documents I am indebted to directors and librarians of the Bancroft Library at Berkeley, the Zimmerman Library at the University of New Mexico, the Lilly Library at the University of Indiana, the Western Historical Collections of Norlin Library at the University of Colorado, the Beinecke Library at Yale University, the Henry E. Huntington Library at San Marino, California, the Western History division of the Denver Public Library, the Stephen H. Hart Library of the Colorado Historical Society, the Penrose Public Library at Colorado Springs, and the Tutt Library at The Colorado College.

Janet Lecompte
Colorado Springs, Colorado

Part 1

Río Arriba, Río Abajo

In 1837, the year of the rebellion, the Department of New Mexico was threatened on all sides by enemies, menaced at her very heart by her own people, and isolated from her only source of aid. New Mexico was on the northern frontier of the Republic of Mexico, sixteen hundred miles and a month of hard travel by fastest courier from the seat of government at Mexico City. Her northern boundary was the Arkansas River, where Americans kept trading posts, sold guns to Plains Indians, and provided a possible base for armed invasion of New Mexico. Her eastern frontier bordered on the new Republic of Texas, whose ambitious leaders claimed New Mexico to the Río Grande del Norte and declared their intentions of invading and securing the claim. On the west were Navajo Indians, who in 1832 had renewed their fierce attacks on the inhabitants after a period of peace. To the south were Gila and Mescalero Apaches who ravaged farms and towns and killed mail carriers, thus breaking the precious thread of communication with Mexico.[1]

The settled part of New Mexico was the valley of the Río Grande del Norte (called Río del Norte or Río Bravo then), which flowed from north to south and cut the department

3

roughly in half. The river was the spine that supported life in this arid land. Its irrigated valleys and those of its little tributaries grew crops of vegetables and fruits, and its barren-looking terraces provided forage for many thousand sheep. As the Río del Norte divided the territory east and west, two districts divided it north and south—Río Arriba and Río Abajo. Río Arriba ("upriver") comprised settlements north of the territorial capital of Santa Fe; Río Abajo ("downriver") lay south of the capital. Santa Fe, although demographically a part of Río Arriba district, was politically neutral, as befits the seat of government. It was situated in the center of the settlements some twenty miles east of the Río del Norte.[2]

Río Arriba was the domain of small farmers and stockmen. They lived in flat-roofed adobe boxes on narrow strips of farmland and pasture, or in fortified villages of adobe houses joined to form hollow squares (plazas). Río Arriba's largest settlement, and in Spanish colonial times a *villa* and administrative center, was Santa Cruz de la Cañada. It was located about twenty miles north of Santa Fe, near the junction of the Santa Cruz River and the Río del Norte. Its population, including a number of smaller villages in the Santa Cruz Valley, was around five thousand souls.[3]

A few miles east of Santa Cruz was (and is) Chimayó, where so many rebels lived in 1837 that the rebellion was sometimes called the "Chimayó Rebellion" and its participants *Chimayoses*. Upstream from Chimayó was Quemado (now Córdoba), still famous for woodcarvers. Farther east was Truchas, its adobe houses strung precariously along the ridge of a narrow foothill of the Sangre de Cristo mountains. The town of Santa Cruz de la Cañada was usually called La Cañada, a word referring either to the dry shallow creek bed of the Santa Cruz River or to the livestock path within it. La Cañada came to refer to the whole region of the Santa

Cruz watershed. In La Cañada, and especially in Chimayó, many of the men were weavers, producing *jerga,* a coarse woolen fabric designed in bold stripes and plaids and used as coats and rugs, and as wrappers for bales of trade goods. The men of La Cañada, particularly those of Chimayó, were distinguished by their plaid coats and braided hair, and were viewed as "rustics" and "half-breeds" by more sophisticated New Mexican society.[4]

Besides its Hispanic villages and villagers (*vecinos*), Río Arriba had nine adobe towns of sedentary Indians who were all Mexican citizens, paying their dues in tithes and military service. The Pueblo Indians were a generally peaceful, if proud and mysterious people, who professed Catholicism and practiced something quite different in the secrecy of their underground kivas. In 1680 the Pueblo Indians joined in a unique cooperative effort and drove the settlers from New Mexico. The memory of this uprising was terrifying to the descendants of these settlers, especially in the tumultuous year of 1837.[5]

Indian pueblos near Santa Fe were Tesuque, Cuyamungué, Nambé, and Pojoaque; pueblos near La Cañada were San Ildefonso, San Juan, Picurís, and Santa Clara. North of La Cañada was a rough mountainous region terminating in the wide and fertile valley of Taos. At the foot of the Sangre de Cristo mountains in the Taos Valley was the many-storied Taos Indian Pueblo and a nearby Hispanic village also called Taos or Don Fernando de Taos. These Taos people, both Hispanic and Indian, were the most independent in all New Mexico. Many were buffalo hunters on the eastern plains and traders with the Plains Indians, and many had Plains Indian blood. Some of the settlers were entirely Indian, captured as children, raised in the Spanish culture, and called *genízaros.* A few Río Arriba settlers were Anglo-Americans

5

or St. Louis Frenchmen; twenty-two of these foreigners lived in the Taos Valley in 1841. A few of the Mexican settlers spent much of their time at American trading posts on the Arkansas River, working as Indian traders or mule packers, or as horse guards for caravans to or from Independence, Missouri. Río Arriba's Plains-Indian and Anglo-American influences were sometimes blamed for the frequent disturbances among its excitable inhabitants. These independent people of Río Arriba outnumbered the conservative populace of Río Abajo by one-third in 1840.[6]

Río Abajo commenced at the southern edge of the broad mesa on which Santa Fe was situated, and stretched south along the Río del Norte past the settlements and through a hundred-mile desert called the *Jornada del Muerto* ("day's journey of the dead man"), to El Paso del Norte (present Ciudad Juárez, Chihuahua). South of El Paso del Norte was more desert, hundreds of miles of it, where water and grass for animals and food and shelter for travelers were scarce, and Indian attacks were frequent. Merchant caravans had to be large and well-guarded to cross this desert safely. Mail carriers were escorted by soldiers, but even so they were often killed and their mail scattered. In the fall of 1837 the mail was discontinued because of Indian attacks. News of the rebellion was carried by a solitary horseman, called an *extraordinario violento*, who galloped over the desert with incredible bravery to keep communications open between Santa Fe and Chihuahua.[7]

Río Abajo was the home of most of the *ricos*, the rich and educated men, the ruling class. They lived in many-roomed adobe houses or walled plazas along with their peons, who tended their houses, fields, orchards, and sheep, and were tied in debt to their masters. In Spanish colonial times, before foreigners were allowed in the country, Río Abajo merchants took caravans south with the products of their land—sheep, blankets, deerskins, buffalo robes, and piñon nuts—but their goods did not sell very well. In those days New Mexico's exports were only half the value of her imports, and nobody got rich. After 1821, when Mexico achieved independence from Spain, American caravans from Missouri flooded New Mexico with fine manufactured goods, and when Río Abajo merchants took these popular goods south, they prospered. The economy of Río Abajo was better than that of Río Arriba, and the Indian pueblos of Río Abajo, except for the more northerly ones of Santo Domingo, Cochití, and Sandía, remained neutral in the rebellion.[8]

Reactions to Neglect

The rebels of 1837 had many complaints, especially regarding the neglect of Mother Mexico. A civil servant, the author of "An Account of the Chimayó Rebellion, 1837" (document 3) declares that "New Mexico, abandoned since the beginning of independence, appeared to have no other relation to the rest of the Republic than a common origin, language, and customs." The abandonment of New Mexico was primarily the result of political upheavals in central Mexico. In the sixteen years between 1821 and 1837, Mexico saw twenty-one turnovers in the office of chief executive, many of them violent. Governmental offices were pervaded with dissention, conspiracy, and corruption, and the public treasury was empty because of constant guerrilla warfare and huge foreign debts. With Mexico chronically on the verge of moral and financial collapse, how could she be expected to support New Mexico's commerce, church, courts, and schools, or to send soldiers and guns?[9]

Although New Mexicans complained constantly, in many

ways they had adjusted to neglect and were not suffering. They were generally poor, but almost every family had some animals and a piece of land. There were few schools, few books, no regular newspapers, but rarely was literacy required of ordinary citizens. The *juez*, or justice of the peace, was often ignorant and sometimes illiterate, but his verdicts were usually sensible and always swift. There were only a dozen priests, and their fees were high: consequently, many people refused to pay the fees and lived without the services and sacraments. [10]

The famous Penitentes were a reaction to neglect. Until 1833, no bishop had visited New Mexico for seventy years, and sacraments requiring dispensation were not performed. The sick often died unconfessed, babies died unbaptized, unmarried couples lived in sin and raised families, and some parishes were visited by priests only a few days in a year. "How resentful must be the poor people who suffer such neglect!" wrote Antonio Barreiro in 1832. The poor were indeed resentful, especially when they paid their tithes and church funds to a church that did not minister to them. In response, a secular brotherhood, Los Hermanos Penitentes, undertook to provide religious ritual and spiritual comfort for the people of Río Arriba. In addition they performed forbidden acts of penitence that included self-flagellation. To the indignation of the populace, Bishop José Antonio de Zubiría declared the cult outlawed when he finally visited New Mexico in 1833. Perhaps remembering the bishop's affront, the people of Río Arriba treated the priests among them with irreverence and abuse during the rebellion four years later. (In 1845, when Bishop Zubiría returned to New Mexico, he found the Penitentes stronger than ever.)[11]

The Misery of the Militia

The truly unbearable part of life in New Mexico, according to Governor Manual Armijo in 1838, was "the continuous war that for more than five consecutive years has been waged with the savage tribes of Navajo." The governor blamed the Navajo war for the ruin of the department and perhaps for the "habitual conspiracy against the government and laws." Losses of life and property through Navajo and Apache attacks on farms and communities were devastating to New Mexicans, but no worse than forced service in the militia. [12]

Since earliest settlement of New Mexico by Europeans, the territory had been surrounded by nomadic and often hostile Indians. Under Spain there had been money for guns, and trained manpower to lead campaigns of militia against the *indios bárbaros,* or to make gifts and play one tribe off against another in the search for peace. Governor Juan Bautista de Anza had made peace with the Comanches in 1786, and for thirty years afterwards these powerful Indians helped protect New Mexico from other Indians. By the 1820s the Comanches had drifted eastward, leaving New Mexico again at the mercy of Navajos, Apaches, and "Indians of the North" (Cheyennes, Arapahos, Kiowa-Apaches). [13]

After 1821, when Mexico achieved independence, money dwindled for guns and ammunition, horses and uniforms, provisions and forage. Gradually the hundred-odd men allotted to Santa Fe's presidial troop shrunk to sixty or seventy ragged soldiers living in dilapidated barracks behind the Governor's Palace, without sufficient guns for each soldier to have one, or enough ammunition for what guns they did have. The soldiers' only functions were to police the streets of Santa Fe, protect the governor, escort caravans of American traders into Santa Fe to prevent smuggling, and search wagons for contraband. In 1835 President Santa Anna ordered that the New Mexico presidial troop be officially reduced to a maximum of seventy men, serving no other purpose than to aid the customs officers.[14]

The main burden of defending New Mexico from Indians had always been borne by the militia, not by the presidial soldiers. The militia were mostly poor farmers and Pueblo Indians, serving under their own officers at their own expense, providing their own guns (more often bows and arrows, clubs, and lances) and their own horses or mules. The share of the spoils they received in battle was inadequate compensation for their losses and for damage done to crops and flocks in their absence. Some men were ruined in a single campaign, trading their family's clothing for ammunition or selling their children into peonage in order to perform their military duty. With every campaign the poor got poorer and more exasperated.[15]

The burden of serving in the militia was never more oppressive than in the 1830s. In the spring of 1833, the rural militia of Río Arriba was called out to fight Navajos. Another Navajo campaign was organized in the fall of 1834, and yet another in February 1835, when Mexican forces were ambushed in a narrow pass and routed. As the Mexicans suffered losses, the Navajos gained booty and confidence. The Indians became so bold that they attacked at the very edge of the settlements, including Santa Fe, stealing stock and children and destroying farms. Farmers were afraid to work in their fields, their crops failed, and hunger threatened the populace.[16]

Such was the misery of the people in May 1835, when Albino Pérez arrived from Mexico to govern New Mexico. In the fall of 1835, the Navajos sued for peace, not liking to make war in winter. The Mexicans did not care for winter campaigns either, and it was the fall of 1836 before Pérez ordered another one. He was unable to gather sufficient soldiers until December 1836, when he left with the rural militia and Pueblo Indian auxiliaries for a two-month winter campaign. The governor's force was meant to be two thousand, but the alcaldes who were ordered to recruit men could obtain only seven hundred and fifty. These were the most poorly clad and hungry wretches in the department, forced to leave their families, farms, and flocks to the mercy of the Plains Indians in order to protect rich men's sheep (or so they viewed the situation). In the bitter weather of an unusually cold winter, they pursued Navajos through the snowy mountains and were rewarded only with the flesh of captured sheep, which they ate, and the pelts, which they wrapped around their legs. Many lost toes and ears to frostbite; one man froze to death. All were mistreated by their rico officers, from whom they suffered insults and refusals of subsistence when they were "dead of hunger".[17]

Governor Pérez expressed to his commanding general his most sincere sympathy for these miserable souls, but the militiamen were unaware of his sympathy and believed him to be the source of their anguish. After this winter campaign, Governor Pérez sent the presidial troops to their homes for lack of funds to maintain them. Gossip spread thereafter that the large salaries and frivolous expenses of the governor's extensive retinue was rapidly depleting the property of the troop and other resources that should have been used to defend the territory from Indians.[18]

Governor Albino Pérez

Albino Pérez probably did not deserve such disrepute as he suffered in New Mexico. He had arrived with an outstanding record as a soldier and with the highest recommendations of character. He was a lieutenant colonel in the Permanent Cavalry; he was considered to be valorous, handsome, and talented, with good connections in the capital that might serve New Mexico well. As governor he had noble, far-sighted plans. He meant to abolish abuses of the old colonial system, control the Navajos, and improve the performance of the troops, which he personally drilled every day. But his good intentions were thwarted by his inexperience with his constituents; he was not a native son, as other recent governors had been, and he lacked first-hand knowledge of the temperament, customs, and concerns of the people.[19]

For instance, Governor Pérez did not understand local politics and underestimated the morality of the people and their representatives when he overlooked the peculation of Francisco Sarracino, a former governor of venal habits. In 1828 Sarracino had been accused of accepting bribes from Spanish priests trying to avoid expulsion from Mexico. In April 1836 he was suspended by Judge Juan Estevan Pino from his position as *subcomisario* (fund-raiser for local government and troops) on charges of defrauding American traders and misapplying public funds. Governor Pérez appointed Manual Armijo in June 1836 to succeed Sarracino. Because of illness, Armijo came to Santa Fe only twice that year from his home in Albuquerque and failed to raise the required funds. In this emergency, Governor Pérez recommended to the Department Assembly on July 15, 1837, that Sarracino be reinstated after the end of the fiscal year, on July 31. Although the Assembly voted five to two in favor of reinstatement, the people disapproved and blamed the governor alone for deliberate disregard of Judge Pino's charges and for unwarranted protection of Sarracino.[20]

Governor Pérez also failed to measure the effect of his sophisticated Mexico City habits upon New Mexico's conservative, provincial society. The governor's own morals probably did not meet local standards. Donaciano Vigil said before the Departmental Assembly, in 1846, that Pérez and his favorites indulged in "orgies," without defining that provocative word in New Mexican terms. Pérez was, at any rate, an adulterer. He had a Mexican wife, Doña Concepción Alarid de Pérez, who remained in Mexico City and received one hundred pesos deducted monthly from his salary. In addition he kept a housekeeper in Santa Fe named Trinidad Trujillo, whose son he fathered. There is no documentary proof that New Mexicans were offended by Pérez's liason with Trinidad. There is considerable evidence, however, that although New Mexicans tolerated concubinage or cohabitation by single persons, adultery was frowned upon, especially when the perpetrator was already the object of envy.[21]

Moreover, Governor Pérez's taste for luxuries and his indifference to the debts he incurred in obtaining them did not please his people. He owned and probably flaunted gorgeous costumes and extravagant appurtenances—velvet pantaloons, a jacket bordered in pure silver with a wide beaver collar, fur capes, several greatcoats (one embroidered in red with the three-star insignia of a colonel's rank), a hat decorated with braid and a cockade, a silver-mounted saddle, and a gold watch worth three hundred pesos (more than most leading citizens of Santa Fe earned in a year). To the crude wood-and-leather furniture in the Governor's Palace he added such exotic pieces as large gilded mirrors borrowed from Francisco Sarracino, a chest of drawers borrowed from Santiago Abréu, a large table clock borrowed from Juan Estevan Pino, and six wooden sofas upholstered in calico. He ordered a fancy two-wheeled carriage and two fine horses worth eight hundred pesos, to be brought from the United States by the Santa Fe trader Jesse Sutton. On campaigns against Indians, he had his choice of two ostentatious camp chairs; one was decorated with silver, the other was of bearskin imported from the United States and worth a hundred pesos. By 1837 the governor was in debt to various natives of New Mexico, to the municipal fund of Santa Fe, to the Post Office, and to American traders (document 1).[22]

American traders in Santa Fe were the source of wealth for New Mexico by 1837. Not only was Governor Pérez in debt to them, but to the government of New Mexico as well. The customs duties that Americans paid on wagonloads of imported goods was the only income the department could count on: it was used to pay the wages and expenses of the presidial troops and civil servants. Some of these American traders were cultivated or useful men who had taken up residence in New Mexico, married New Mexicans, and contributed their talents and skills as well as their money and military service to their adopted land. Others were shameless smugglers, and their teamsters were rough and rowdy frontiersmen, always armed, often drunk, and the source of trouble at dances and public gatherings.[23]

However much Mexicans detested these Americans, they usually treated them with respect. One of the complaints against Governor Pérez was that he did not prevent his treasury officers from harassing American traders who had extended them credit or made loans to the government of New Mexico against the amount of their customs duties. In July 1837, as the Americans were ready to leave with their wagons for the United States, treasury employees refused to pay back their loans on various excuses, and were seen gambling away amounts equal to them. At last the traders had to leave for the United States without collecting the money due them. Most of the creditors were from Taos, and their mistreatment at the hands of the treasury officers reinforced the calumnies spreading in Río Arriba against the governor.[24]

Thus was Governor Pérez blamed for conditions that were not altogether his fault—the miseries of the militia, the appointment of the suspended Sarracino, and the irresponsibility of the treasury officers. He was also criticized for things that might be considered no one else's business—his choice of friends, clothes, and private entertainment (the so-called orgies). Some of Pérez's most strongly censured actions certainly were public business, but not everyone disapproved of them. In 1835 Governor Pérez appointed as prefect the former subcomisario Ramón Abréu, a citizen who had spent all his adult life in public service and was undoubtedly competent. Other aspirants for the job, who believed they should have been preferred for their seniority, wealth, and prestige, began to spread destructive rumors about Abréu, hoping to harass him into resigning. They whispered that the unjust municipal taxes recently imposed by authorities of Santa Fe were instigated by Pérez and served as a sample of what the governor meant to accomplish on a larger scale. They even accused the Pérez government of inventing the constitutional law of Mexico along with its taxes, in order to rob the people of New Mexico with an appearance of legality.[25]

In a speech before the Departmental Assembly, nine years later, Donaciano Vigil accused these rumor mongers of planning the revolution:

As soon as the common people were raised to a certain level of discontent, distrust, and exaltation by this means, the tenacious enemies of Señor Pérez planned a revolution that had for its ostensible object only the jobs of the present favorites of Señor Pérez.

Intending at first no more than to ask Señor Pérez for these, they joined the more excited people at various points in Río Arriba. Señor Pérez knew perfectly well the authors of these movements and the object that they had in mind, which was to destroy him and all his employees, but underestimating the movers and their means, he persisted in following the counsel of his favorites.[26]

Not only the excited populace but also the Departmental Assembly now saw the need to get rid of Pérez. That body drew up a *terna*, or list of three nominees, from which the Supreme Government would choose the next governor—but Albino Pérez's name was not on it. Pérez raised objections and suggested that the Assembly draw up another list, but with both the people and their government against him, Pérez's future in New Mexico was precarious.[27]

The Departmental Plan

After Mexico achieved independence in 1821, the people of New Mexico enjoyed fourteen years of democratic freedoms. In 1833 the governor of New Mexico wrote that "the ideas of liberty have been spread even among the most ignorant and remote people." Donaciano Vigil recalled those joyous times:

As soon as the glorious independence of the Mexican nation was proclaimed, New Mexico embraced it with great enthusiasm. Delightful theories sprung up, and patriotic discussions circulated among us, promising us an era of happiness and liberty—these two words were much used then, and echoed far and wide. All of us, in those times, were tinted with the color of rose (document 2).[28]

The color of rose turned ashen in 1836, with the advent of President Antonio López Santa Anna's centralist government. Santa Anna abolished the 1824 constitution, which was based on that of the United States, and substituted a new constitutional law of December 29, 1836, known as the Siete Leyes ("seven laws"), or Departmental Plan. Its effect was to centralize all branches of government, make laws uniform throughout the Republic, and weaken local self-government. The Plan benefited Santa Anna and central Mexico, but it was born of the desperation of a nation so weakened internally that only by tightening the collar and shortening the leash could it hope to keep its far-flung provinces at heel. The provinces reacted violently; revolutionary movements broke out in Zacatecas, Sonora, Sinaloa, Tamaulipas, Yucatán, Coahuila, and California. Rebels in these departments were brought to order with federal troops or the threat of them. Rebels in Texas, mostly Anglo-Saxons, fought to the death at the Alamo early in 1836 and finally defeated Santa Anna and his army at San Jacinto, to win their independence.[29]

In New Mexico the most offensive measure of the Departmental Plan was the decree that federal taxes would be collected equally in all departments. New Mexicans had never paid a direct federal tax, because of military service performed by the citizens; nor had it received its share of federal benefits—troops and arms, schools and hospitals, roads and bridges. The constitutional law of December 29, 1836, was not the direct cause of New Mexico's revolt, for it stated only that every citizen must contribute to the expenses of government, and New Mexicans assumed that as usual they would be exempt from such contributions. What raised havoc in New Mexico was a law of April 17, 1837, defining the political apparatus for collecting and distributing taxes.

Because of New Mexico's great distance from the capital, Governor Pérez did not receive, or at least acknowledge receipt of, a copy of the latter law until July 8, 1837. The people of New Mexico probably did not fully comprehend that they were in danger of being taxed until after July 10, when Pérez called the acting subcomisario Ambrosio Armijo into his office to discuss the law of April 17, 1837, and the collection of taxes.[30]

Even then the governor probably had no intention of imposing taxes on his unwilling constituents. According to the anonymous author of "An Account of the Chimayó Rebellion":

Informed of the public opinion in general and particularly with respect to taxes, or rather believing that the Supreme Government would exempt New Mexico from being a department and from paying taxes because of the peculiarity of its situation and its poverty, the governor took no steps to collect taxes nor even to consider the matter, fearing no doubt that it would cause some popular commotion (little did he know how much!) and he awaited the resolution of the Supreme Government.[31]

Nevertheless, absurd rumors began to circulate among the people that the tax would amount to half a family's property, or to a "third of the fruits of their labor, the common benefits of water, wood, pasture, and even their own children and wives."[32]

While Governor Pérez was discussing taxes with his subcomisario in July 1837, the people of Santa Cruz de la Cañada were organizing a revolt in Río Arriba. They later claimed the threat of taxes as their motivation, but in fact other threats to their freedom and dignity affected them more immediately.

Cantón at La Cañada

In December 1836, most of the seven members of La Cañada's *ayuntamiento,* or municipal council, were found to be related, an illegal but far from unusual situation in towns where only a few families were well enough educated to serve as councilmen. In strict observance of the law, Governor Pérez dissolved the ayuntamiento and ordered new elections, infuriating the people of La Cañada. At the same time, a man named Antonio Abad Montoya, who was related to the alcalde and to most of the councilmen, was put in jail for what was described at Santa Fe as "a grave crime." Montoya appealed to the governor, who advised him that his sole right of appeal was to the Supreme Court of the nation. In February 1837 Montoya determined on a quicker way out of jail and bribed his relative, the alcalde Juan José Esquibel, to set him free without bond. The governor ordered Montoya to be returned immediately to jail and Alcalde Esquibel to be punished with a fifty-peso fine. The alcalde disobeyed the governor's order and defied the law—no jail for Montoya, no fine for Esquibel![33]

This was not the only time Alcalde Esquibel flouted authority. In his alcalde court he heard the complaint of Víctor Sánchez of Taos, who had paid customs duties in the City of Chihuahua for two men of La Cañada, and who had a document to prove it. When the two men refused to pay Sánchez, Alcalde Esquibel supported them. Sánchez complained to the governor, who sent him to the prefect, Ramón Abréu. Prefect Abreu ordered the alcalde to render justice to Sánchez, but the alcalde disobeyed. Abréu suspended Esquibel, and when Antonio Abad Montoya's bribe came to light, Abréu ordered Esquibel arrested, jailed, and placed in irons. At the end of July 1837, a mob at La Cañada freed

Esquibel, who then declared himself an enemy of the authorities. Forming a twelve-member council that he named Cantón ("district," or "neighborhood"), he proceeded to organize a rebellion.[34]

On August 1 Esquibel and his rebel followers issued a proclamation showing that their anger was not simply at the jailing of their alcalde, but also at the Departmental Plan, its taxes, and the extravagance of the governor and his clique:

Long live God and the Nation and the faith of Jesus Christ, for the most important issues they stand for are following:
1. To sustain God and the nation and the faith of Jesus Christ.
2. To defend our country until the last drop of blood is shed to achieve the desired victory.
3. Not to allow the Departmental Plan.
4. Not to allow any tax.
5. Not to allow the excesses of those who try to carry this out.
God and the Nation, Santa Cruz de la Cañada, August 1, 1837, in camp.[35]

As a statement of policy, the proclamation lacked eloquence, but as a rallying cry it was effective. After its publication, Alcalde Esquibel and his Cantón set about wooing the people of Río Arriba to their cause. Their enemies asserted that the Cantón spread lies about the Pérez administration and invented laws, orders, and letters that they pretended were intercepted from the authorities. It was said that in a Cantón meeting the rebels decided to demand that Pérez deliver up for execution his secretary, Jesús María Alarid, district Judge Santiago Abréu, and the prefect of the first district, Ramón Abréu. The rebels were influenced, as rumor had it, by those who meant to slide into the vacancies thus created. After a few days of lies, invented laws, and hard work, the rebels collected an army and used it to force others to join their cause.[36]

Rebel resistance was not only to the Departmental Plan and its proponents, but also to the restrictions imposed by the church and priests. Padre Fernando Ortiz, priest of Santa Cruz, wrote two months later that the conspiracy in La Cañada was kept so secret that he did not know it existed until a few days before it erupted in revolt. The rebels gathered at Santa Cruz in increasing numbers and decided quickly on a list of demands. Some of their demands involved the church: priests should expect no contributions except *primicias* (the early yield of fields and flocks), and burials should be permitted inside the church (which was against the law). In the Santa Cruz sanctuary, Padre Ortiz was forced to perform such burials with a gun at his back. He wrote that the rebels committed other mortifications to his person and to the church, too numerous to detail. One night Indians of the Taos and San Ildefonso pueblos apprehended the padre and were about to drag him off to the *reunión,* or meeting of rebels, but were deterred by the persuasion of an Indian friend of the priest, from San Ildefonso. Any resistance to the reunión, wrote Padre Ortiz, was fraught with danger and sometimes ended in death.[37]

Battle at La Mesilla

Word of the La Cañada insurrection and a copy of the rebel proclamation had reached Santa Fe by August 2. On that day Governor Pérez announced that he would march for Santa Cruz at four in the afternoon with members of the Departmental Assembly, to have a talk with the dissidents. He wrote his military commander, Lieutenant Colonel José María Ronquillo, denouncing the rebels and their "frivolous pretext" for rebelling, and putting Ronquillo in charge of both civil and military government of the Department and of the city of Santa Fe. Then Pérez prepared to go forth with all his civil officers and extinguish the little flame of sedition that flickered at La Cañada.[38]

Pérez did not march for La Cañada on August 2 as he intended, however, probably because he learned that the trouble was not with a handful of malcontents but with a civil uprising of major proportion. According to the historian Benjamin Read, Pérez was advised to leave New Mexico in haste to save his life, but he chose to stay.[39]

While the Cantón was preparing Río Arriba for full-scale revolt, the governor wasted precious time, believing in spite of many warnings that the rebels posed no danger. When he tried to collect a force for subduing them, he found few men willing to serve. Many protested illness or press of business; alcaldes charged with recruiting men failed to present more than small parties. On August 5 some Pueblo Indian recruits arrived from Río Abajo, and Pérez sent a swift messenger to Río Abajo to collect more men. On that same day, the governor issued a proclamation that at the ringing of a bell or firing of a cannon, men should gather with their arms in the Santa Fe plaza, ready to march.[40]

On August 7 Governor Pérez set out for La Cañada with about two hundred militiamen, mostly Pueblo Indians from the Río Abajo pueblos of Cochití, Santo Domingo, and Sandía, serving under officers of the Santa Fe presidial troops, including Lieutenant Colonel Manuel Aponte, Lieutenant Manuel Hurtado, Alférez Diego Sáenz, and Alférez Ramón Baca. Among other presidials in the force were Corporal Tomás Martínez, Corporal Manuel Maldonado, and the soldiers José Sena, Nepomoceno Jiménez, and Juan Sandoval. For purposes of negotiation, Pérez brought along members

Detail from Miera-Pacheco's 1779 map of New Mexico. A magnifying glass will reveal Santa Fe ("Sta Fee, Cap^l y Precidio,") Tesuque, "Pujuaque" and "S. Ildefonso" along Pérez's route to disaster. (Museum of New Mexico #51172).

Top: The Santa Cruz valley showing the church of Nuestra Señora de Carmel y San Francisco at Santa Cruz de la Cañada (Museum of New Mexico #102247).

This view of Santa Cruz is taken from the south tower belfry of the Church of Nuestra Señora de Carmel y San Francisco (New Mexico State Museum #1304.27, copy courtesy of the Taylor Museum, Colorado Springs Fine Arts center).

Chimayó and the Santa Cruz valley (Colorado Historical Society).

Truchas, home of rebel Antonio Vigil, pictured in about 1935 with
lumber from the nearby mountains (photo by T. Harmon Parkhurst,
Museum of New Mexico #9048).

Córdova, a rebel village (Harrington Collection, Albuquerque Museum-UNM Joint Photographic Project, Zimmerman Library, UNM).

Taos Pueblo (Colorado Historical Society).

La Mesilla or Black Mesa, where Pérez's forces were routed on August 8, 1837. In the foreground is the Pueblo of San Ildefonso and Pojoaque Creek, and at the left center a bend of the Rio Grande (aerial photo by Tyler Dingee, c. 1950, Museum of New Mexico #74174).

Top: "GOVERNOR PÉREZ was assassinated on this s[pot] Aug. 9, 1837." So says the D.A.R. marker of 1901, which is now in the patio of the Governor's Palace in Santa Fe. (photo c. 1954, Museum of New Mexico #51124).

Rosario Chapel at Santa Fe. Here the rebels camped on the night of August 10, 1837 (Museum of New Mexico #10062).

of his government—District Court Judge Santiago Abréu, Prefect Ramón Abréu, Departmental Secretary Jesús María Alarid, Subcomisario Francisco Sarracino, First Alcalde of Santa Fe Agustín Durán, Second Alcalde of Santa Fe Felipe Sena, and other citizens. Pérez had no intention of doing battle with the rebels; he meant only to appease them, and his little army and two cannon were merely for protection of the civil officers.[41]

Pérez's route appears to have been the road to La Cañada that went northwest of Santa Fe through woods and Cañadas. Beyond the Indian pueblo of Tesuque, eight miles north of Santa Fe, the trees and gullies gave way to sandy flatlands interspersed with "broken and troublesome little hills," as Fray Domínguez described it in 1776. There Pérez turned west to Pojoaque, where the party camped for the night. The next morning he continued west to the Indian pueblo of San Ildefonso, on the Río del Norte, and started north along the river around buttes and over broken terrain. On the left side of the road, two miles north of the San Ildefonso plaza, a black butte called La Mesilla (known now as Black Mesa) rose six hundred feet above the river bank. From La Mesilla the road ran north in sight of the Río del Norte and after eight miles came to Santa Cruz de la Cañada.[42]

Governor Pérez never got as far as Santa Cruz. At La Mesilla the governor and his forces met four factions of rebels, fifteen hundred to two thousand strong. As he prepared to negotiate, one of the enemy factions began firing rapidly, and soon all were firing in wild disorder. When the rebels attacked, the Indians with Pérez deserted and joined the enemy in attacking the governor's party. Two of Pérez's militia officers, ten soldiers, and two citizens of Santa Fe also deserted, taking with them one of the cannon, after cutting the ropes and harness of the mules drawing it. Francisco

Sarracino, in charge of the governor's vanguard, hastily retreated to the remaining cannon, which Sergeant Donaciano Vigil had positioned at the top of a hill. Colonel Pérez came up and exclaimed, "Sarracino, my friend, don't abandon the cannon!" Sarracino answered, "Have no fear—I would sooner abandon my life than the cannon!" But the tumult became so great that no one had time to load the cannon. Pérez and his few remaining soldiers shot at the enemy from the top of the hill with only their muskets, until rebels climbed the hill from the opposite side and killed six men guarding the cannon. Then Pérez and twenty-three faithful men fled south.[43]

The rebels captured most of the rest of his soldiers—Alférez Ramón Baca, Sergeant Donaciano Vigil, Corporal Tomás Martínez, Corporal Manuel Maldonado, the soldiers José Sena, Nepomocena Jiménez, and Juan Sandoval, along with the wounded Francisco Sarracino and the civilians Agustín Durán, Felipe Sena, and Juan Bustamante. The prisoners were disarmed, stripped of their clothing and other property, and manacled with rawhide. Then they were led on foot to the prison at Santa Cruz, where they were detained for five or six days.[44]

Donaciano Vigil was the only captive not manacled and jailed at Santa Cruz. Vigil never explained in the records why he received such preferential treatment. His behavior was the subject of an investigation in January 1838, which established that he had been entirely loyal to Pérez during the battle, but after his capture he had been asked by Antonio Abad Montoya to act as secretary and scribe for the Cantón, and he had agreed to do so. He probably had little choice.[45]

The victory of the rebels over Governor Pérez was the subject of popular songs, or *décimas*. One décima wryly celebrated Donaciano Vigil's appointment:

The people again come out
With great excitement and noise
Because victory has perched
With the alcalde of La Cañada;

And because they are such boors
That they cannot even write,
They have appointed as secretary
Don Donaciano Vigil.[46]

Pérez and his men escaped to Santa Fe, arriving on the afternoon of August 8. They set off again at ten o'clock that night, Pérez on his spotted horse, El Buen Amigo. The party consisted of the governor; the three Abréu brothers, Santiago, Ramón, and the schoolmaster Marcelino; Secretary of Government Jesús María Alarid; Alférez Diego Sáenz of the presidial troop; Miguel Sena of the Río Abajo militia; militia Lieutenant José (or Joaquín, or Manuel) Hurtado; the militiaman José Loreto Escobar (or Escoto, or Soto, or Loreto Romero, as he was variously remembered); and a man named Ortega. On the way they met a force of militia under the rebel A. Antonito Chávez, who refused them protection, and they turned back towards Santa Fe. The rebels had already sent instructions to Santo Domingo Pueblo that Pérez was headed south. As Pérez and his party approached the house of an old man called Tío Salvadorito (Salvador Martínez), on Agua Fría road southwest of Santa Fe, (and now within the city limits), the Santo Domingo Indians overtook them.[47]

Governor Pérez resisted with all his might. When his horse was killed under him, he continued to fight with his pistols, and when he ran out of ammunition, he fought with only his dagger, killing several of his assailants. After he was wounded and brought to the ground, the Indians were still afraid to get close to him, and they shot him from a distance.

They cut off his head and carried it on a pole to the rebel camp near the church of Nuestra Señora del Rosario, in Santa Fe. Keeping up a continual shouting, the rebels would yell at Pérez's head, "Ah, you robber! You will no longer extort taxes; you will no longer drink chocolate or coffee!" They kicked the head about with their spurred heels, hacked it with their sabers, and stuck it with their arrows. They threatened with death anyone who buried the naked, headless body of the governor, or attempted to clothe the corpse. After the new government was installed, Albino Chacón obtained permission to bury the body. Late on the night of August 10, Chacón hastily dug a grave in the city graveyard and buried the disorderly remains of the governor, which were clad only in undergarments.[48]

Other members of Pérez's party scattered in different directions, every man for himself. Santiago Abréu was captured near Cerrillos on August 8 and was carried to Santo Domingo Pueblo, where he was kept in the stocks overnight. The next day he was killed by having his members cut off one at a time and shaken in his face. Jesús María Alarid was dragged from his house, stripped, and lanced to death; others received similar treatment. All the bodies were left exposed to birds and beast of prey until some Christian buried them.[49]

Seventeen men died, six of them soldiers killed during the battle. Three were wounded, including Lieutenant Colonel José Manuel Aponte, who hid in a house in Santa Fe. The rebels ordered the authorities of Santa Fe to find Aponte; when they found him, the owner of the house delivered him up to the rebels. Soldiers and citizens of Santa Fe witnessed this surrender with helpless shame and indignation (but Aponte survived both his wounds and his capture).[50]

Rebels Rampant

On August 10 the main body of rebels approached Santa Fe
from the north and were met by Lieutenant Colonel José
María Ronquillo, to whom Pérez had entrusted the government in his absence. Ronquillo marched out to meet the
rebels bearing a white flag, congratulating them and putting himself at their service. He was later denounced as a
traitor for this act, but it may have deterred the rebels from
sacking the city, as the inhabitants had anticipated. The
rebels went directly to the parroquia, or parish church, to
offer up thanks to God for their victory. Then they camped
that night near the church of the Rosario, five hundred yards
from the Santa Fe plaza.[51]

The Santa Fe traders in Santa Fe, numbering about two
hundred at that time, according to Carl Blumner, prepared
for a rebel attack. In front of their shops, facing the plaza,
they assembled with not fewer than five or six hundred loaded
guns. In nearby courtyards and stables they kept their horses
and mules saddled for a quick escape. But all went quietly;
Josiah Gregg, an American trader then on his way to El Paso
del Norte, writes that the rebels molested neither the inhabitants of Santa Fe nor a caravan of American merchants there.
Other American traders reported to a St. Louis newspaper
that the Americans "had not been molested, but there was
no security for their property, and one of them had been
marked for sacrifice—which one would not be known until
his head was seen on a pole!" A native of Santa Fe contra-
dicted Gregg in saying that the rebels committed "numberless
robberies upon us all."[52]

At camp on August 10, the rebels acclaimed as governor
José Gonzales, who with Rafael García had commanded the
rebel force. The rebels carried the new governor through

the streets of Santa Fe in a sedan chair, shouting "Long live Christ, and death to the robbers!" Then they all returned to camp and proceeded to divide up the property of those they had killed. The principal beneficiaries were the most active of the rebels. Two of them, who claimed to be creditors of the dead men, received jewels. The rebel who had been distinguished for outrages against the head of Pérez was rewarded with the governor's bloody dolman, a cloak with wide sleeves, which he put on, strutting about and displaying the hole made by the bullet that killed the governor. The next day the rebels went home, leaving José Gonzales at the Governor's Palace to fulfill the nebulous aims expressed in the pronouncement at Santa Cruz. From this day on, the people of New Mexico, and particularly those of Santa Fe, lived in a state of confusion and terror, with no more law in force than the wishes of the friends of the governor and of the Cantón.[53]

Governor José Gonzales

In a land of many distinct and largely unblended cultures—Mexican, Pueblo Indian, Plains Indian, Anglo-American—it has become a matter of interest to know a man's ethnic composition. New Mexico had abandoned the castes that served this purpose in colonial times. After independence any respectable man was allowed the title of *don*, and modern historians must look elsewhere to identify a man's race and culture. José Gonzales's background, therefore, has become a matter of some importance and speculation.

Over the years José Gonzales has been successively identified as: a vecino of the village of Taos; an Indian from the Taos Pueblo; and a genízaro living in San Francisco del Rancho (now Ranchos de Taos). His Hispanic contemporaries knew him as one of themselves, a vecino with no more than the ordinary admixture of Indian blood; in contemporary accounts of the rebellion no one suggested that he was anything else. Twenty years later, in his popular book *El Gringo*, W. H. H. Davis called him a Taos Indian, on what evidence or misunderstanding we can only guess. A century of historians followed Davis in wrapping José Gonzales in the blanket of an Indian—in 1883 L. Bradford Prince, in 1912 Ralph Emerson Twitchell, in 1962 Warren A. Beck. In 1955 José Gonzales was declared a genízaro, and recent historians have uncritically accepted this identification. But the two writers who called Gonzales a Taos Indian or genízaro produced no credible evidence for their assumptions. It is probably safer to say, with the governor's contemporaries, that he was a vecino.[54]

Rafael Chacón, writing at the turn of the century, claimed José Gonzales as a relative:

They had appointed as their provisional governor one José Gonzales, a good and worthy man, who was a first cousin to Don Rafael Páez, my father-in-law. Some American historians deriving their information from unreliable sources, have stated this man was a Pueblo Indian, evidently from the fact that the Indians took a very active part in this uprising: but this assertion is not true; Señor Gonzales was a pure creole of Spanish blood, of good and respectable appearance; he was a peaceful and worthy citizen who was made the tool for the ambition of others who were more worldy-wise than himself. He had the reputation of being a first class buffalo-hunter, an accomplishment which in those days was held in great esteem, and he who excelled in it was always taken for a brave and honorable man.[55]

Peaceful and worthy, brave and honorable, and a first-class buffalo hunter he undoubtedly was, but for his own faction to make him leader in battle and governor afterwards, he must have been more than that. Perhaps he was the José Gonzales of Taos who was one of twelve outstanding militia commanders of whom two were to be chosen for a campaign against the Apaches in 1834, and one of five commanders of militia under Governor Pérez on the Navajo campaign during the winter of 1836–37, for which the governor gave him a citation. But if José Gonzales were this well-known citizen-soldier, why would his contemporaries not mention the fact?[56]

By the time José Gonzales was acclaimed governor, news of the rebellion was already on its way south to Mexico and northeast to Missouri, carried by caravans of American merchants. At eight o'clock on the night of August 4, American and Mexican traders left Santa Fe hurriedly for El Paso del Norte. As they passed through the Río Abajo towns, they found the people generally in agreement with the rebel cause. On their way they were joined by other merchants with reports from Santa Fe about the battle and the murder of the governor and his officers. The merchants reached El Paso on August 28 with their news and were detained several hours by the military commander, Lieutenant Colonel Cayetano Justiniani, while their statements were taken. The statements were sent immediately by extraordinario violento to Mexico City. They were read to the Mexican Congress on September 11 and published in the September 12 issue of the government's official newspaper, *Diario del Gobierno de la República Mexicana*. The statements of the merchants were quoted in their entirety.[57]

In the meantime another caravan of American traders left Santa Fe, on August 12, for Independence, Missouri, a journey of about forty days. On October 2 a St. Louis newspaper published a trader's account of the rebellion, probably the first account to reach the United States.[58]

José Gonzales's first act as governor was to issue a proclamation begging his people to be patient with his shortcomings:

The governor of New Mexico to his fellow-citizens: By the general wish of the inhabitants I have been named their governor. In such critical circumstances as our beloved homeland finds itself, I can do no less than happily assent to the high position in which the people have placed me, through no merit on my part. Well do I know, my fellow-citizens, the insufficiency of my learning for the duty I must discharge, and I hope that everyone will be patient with my faults which, whatever else they may be, will not be that of malice, and if they be from lack of knowledge, I hope I can be pardoned by my fellow-citizens and friends. Santa Fe, August 11, 1837.[59]

José Gonzales's statement was admirably candid and modest, but it was not politically astute and did not inspire confidence in his leadership. Josiah Gregg testified at El Paso del Norte, in August 1837, that Gonzales was "an idiot neither worthy nor capable of keeping the position he usurped." Later, in *Commerce of the Prairies*, Gregg amended his statement to read that Gonzales was "without civil virtues and so ignorant that he was unable even to sign his own name." The author of "An Account of the Chimayó Rebellion" wrote that Gonzales was a farmer, "whose only talent was knowing how to kill buffalo." W. H. H. Davis wrote that he was "a good honest hunter but a very ignorant man."[60]

On August 11 reports arrived that rebels were about to invade Santa Fe to commit more outrages. After issuing his statement, José Gonzales immediately departed, presumably to calm the rebels of La Cañada. On his return he began to function as chief executive, with the help of Secretary Donaciano Vigil, Treasurer Vicente Sánchez Vergara, and Assistant Military Inspector and Commander of Troops Lieutenant Colonel José María Ronquillo. First Gonzales combined the offices of administrator of revenue, held by Sánchez Vergara, and subcomisario, held by Francisco Sarracino, into one office of treasurer, under Sánchez Vergara, thus eliminating the controversial Sarracino, whose appointment by Pérez had so nettled the people. Next Gonzales appointed Francisco Baca y Terrus as subcomisario.[61]

Then Governor Gonzales suggested an imaginative if startling way to circumvent the Departmental Plan. He issued an invitation to various foreigners to join his cause, march to the United States, and offer to annex New Mexico to that nation. When Gonzales proposed this scheme to Elisha Stanley, long-time American trader and resident of Santa Fe, Stanley "did not care to accede to it," and the idea was abandoned. But patriots of New Mexico would not forget it. Manuel Armijo later referred to Gonzales's proposition when he wrote of a traitorous attempt to "rend the national flag by substituting the shameful symbol of foreign domination."[62]

A Disastrous *Junta Popular*

Near the end of August, Governor Gonzales prepared to send representatives to Mexico City, to voice the grievances of the rebels and the concerns of the new government. He invited important men of the Department to meet in Santa Fe on August 27 to choose delegates, and he asked Santa Clara and Tesuque pueblos to provide four men for escorting the delegates to Mexico. The priest of Tomé, Padre Francisco Ignacio Madariaga, sent his regret that illness prevented him from attending a meeting "for a purpose as reasonable as you propose." Padre Antonio José Martínez of Taos attended the meeting after celebrating Mass (with a Te Deum for the soul of Albino Pérez) at Chimayó at the invitation of the rebel alcalde Juan José Esquibel. Padre Martínez's early sympathy with the rebels later gave rise to the suspicion that he was part of the original conspiracy, if there was one.[63]

The priest was not the only important man to support the rebels in the beginning. In August Governor Gonzales and his "reasonable" purposes gained the support of many New Mexicans, not only the Río Arriba rebels who elected him governor, but also some educated and well-off men who hated the centralist Departmental Plan and opposed the unfortunate Governor Pérez, who was duty-bound to carry it out. Besides Padre Martínez, and probably Padre Madariaga, citizens who were apparently not hostile to Gonzales included Donaciano Vigil and Vicente Sánchez Vergara who became Gonzales's chief advisors, and Lieutenant Colonel Ronquillo, who went out from Santa Fe to greet the triumphant rebel forces and fled the city when the opposition gained the upper hand. In favor of the rebel stand were most of the people that Juan García met in Río Abajo as he traveled south with the caravan and the citizens of Santa Fe who had deserted Pérez at the start of the battle. Governor Gonzales had an early constituency of respectable men, although many of his later partisans were motivated only by terror of the Cantón.[64]

However strong Governor Gonzales's support, it was to evaporate after the meeting on August 27 to elect representatives for Mexico. Early that morning, before the meeting convened, Governor Gonzales divided up among his supporters the property found in the houses of massacre victims, which left families of victims destitute and their creditors without recourse. Among the creditors were American merchants of Santa Fe. These merchants sent a memorial to the American legation at Mexico City. The memorial stated that Gonzales's distribution of property was sanctioned by a general meeting of alcaldes and principal men who solemnly approved all the acts of the victorious party, including the murder of government officers, election of the governor, and division of property of the dead men. Because of this official sanction of the property distribution, the merchants claimed compensation for damages, not from the outlaw mob but from the Republic of Mexico.[65]

Minutes of the meeting indicate no specific approval of the acts of the mob such as the merchants described in their memorial. The minutes taken by Secretary Donaciano Vigil show that citizens invited to the *junta popular* met under the *portal* of the Governor's Palace from August 27 to 30. They spent these days composing an explanation for the murder of Pérez and his associates and deciding how to present it to the Supreme Government. According to a portion of the minutes:

Colonel Pérez's unfortunate death was because of his not granting the request to remove his secretary Jesús María Alarid, the prefect Ramón Abréu, named at Pérez's whim, and the district judge Santiago Abréu from their illegally held offices, and because of Pérez's usurpation of the full power of all these offices, which should derive from the fundamental laws dictated by the Supreme Government. For the individual security of the inhabitants, entire obedience will be given to the Supreme Government as always, and in proof of this it is agreed that the voice of the people and no other can repair the damage done by Señor Pérez and his wicked subordinates who tried to impose arbitrary taxes that would serve only to enrich themselves.[66]

After more discussion of a lively and controversial nature, as revealed by much deletion and revision in the minutes, four propositions were presented (and later withdrawn): (1) that the authority of Governor Pérez be denied; (2) that the appointment of José Gonzales as governor be approved; (3) that commissioners be authorized to present the desperate circumstances of New Mexico to the Supreme Government; and (4) that these commissioners should be the curate Antonio José Martínez, Manual Armijo, and the alcalde Juan José Esquibel. The three commissioners were to be summoned to the palace at three o'clock the next afternoon to sign their acceptance. For some reason not apparent in the minutes, these four propositions were struck out with three bold strokes of a quill pen. No evidence exists that Martínez, Armijo, and Esquibel were appointed, that they agreed to serve, or that Armijo and Esquibel were even present at the meeting, although Martínez was.[67]

The minutes of the next day's meeting are the roughest of notes, interlined, amended with textual and marginal comments, patched and scratched with additions and deletions. They indicate a contentious discussion concerning what should be told to the Supreme Government, whether two commissioners should go to Mexico, or whether (as one deduces from scraps of crossed out phrases) the message should go by *extraordinario violento*. After stating that all members of the junta popular should be present the next morning to elect the commissioners by a majority vote, the whole paragraph was struck out, again in heavy, broad strokes from the pen of the frustrated secretary. On the third day the junta agreed that the governor ought not to be subject to established laws, but to circumstances as they arose. He should, however, respect federal laws until the commissioners could inform the Supreme Government of the causes of the revolt and ask for laws "analogous" to New Mexico. So ended the meeting, without achieving its principal object of choosing representatives.[68]

Rebel Aims Revealed

In the minutes of the junta popular we hear rebel voices more clearly than in any other document, and we begin to understand what they wanted. The rebel statement that Pérez held his office illegally because he was not chosen by the people seems to be incongruous with the rebel declaration of loyalty to the Supreme Government, of which those they murdered were legal representatives. But there was apparently no incongruity in rebel minds, for they simply rejected the 1836 constitution along with its central control, its governors, its prefects, and its taxes, and proposed to be governed by the democratic 1824 constitution.[69]

Rebel aims were not well defined. Doubtless some rebels thought New Mexico should go the way of Texas and declare independence, or offer allegiance to the United States as Governor Gonzales had proposed. Some did not want independence from Mexico but liberty within its political boundaries, although most appeared to equate freedom with anarchy: Manuel Armijo wrote that "the aim of the factions was, as is evident, to remain independent of the Mexican nation . . . and to live without subjection to any law or authority." The junta popular proposed that the governor ought not to be subject to established laws; José Caballero echoed the phrase in describing the rebels as "disclaiming all the laws and constitution." The most radical rebels thought all civil officers not elected by the people were serving unconstitutionally and deserved to die, a rationalization for the murder of Pérez and his civil officers.[70]

The rebellion was not a class or race war, not poor against rich, nor Río Arriba against Río Abajo, nor Indian against white, although these tensions existed. In August of 1837, rich and poor stood together against the moral and financial excesses of Pérez; Río Abajo in general supported the Río Arriba rebels' democratic aims as they were then understood; Indians and vecinos fought together on the battlefield.

The rebellion failed not because the rebels lacked initial support, but because they lacked unity among themselves and a strong and logical statement of purpose. They also lacked an audacious leader to see that their aims were realized. They had no such leader in José Gonzales, who would run his department not by established laws but by circumstances as they arose, and would be lost and bewildered in either the anarchy or despotism that resulted. It was probably at the junta popular that wiser heads, even those who had sympathized with the goals of the rebels and had overlooked their brutality, decided to rid New Mexico of the rebel governor and his government. And it was probably at this meeting that the Cantón also decided that José Gonzales was not its choice for governor after all.

On September 2, Governor Gonzales called another meeting of what might be called his cabinet—himself, Colonel Ronquillo, and Secretary Vigil—to appoint men of "integrity, purity, business acumen and prudence" as "legal deputies of all the citizens of the Department" for which (as the minutes protested several times) this little junta had ample legal power. Appointed as deputies were Antonio José Martínez and Vicente Sánchez Vergara, who were to travel to Mexico and present to both houses of congress "the evils of Governor Pérez and associates, and express the entire obedience of the Department to the Supreme Government." The deputies were also to describe the lack of resources and the misery of the inhabitants and to beg for the revocation of present laws and the passage of laws beneficial to the Department.[71]

With the help of Donaciano Vigil, Sánchez Vergara, and Ronquillo (his chief and perhaps only advisors), Governor Gonzales was obviously trying to establish lawful government; but the blood on his hands made it difficult. Deputies to Mexico might have had some trouble demonstrating that a faction that had just murdered the government's legal representatives was in "entire obedience" to that government. In any case, the deputies never left for Mexico. Padre Antonio José Martínez was not in Santa Fe when he was appointed and probably knew nothing about it, and Sánchez Vergara was already working secretly against Governor Gonzales, as we shall see.

The Cantón that had elected José Gonzales no longer supported his moderate goals, and, contrary to expectation, refused to be dissolved. In the same angry spirit that had impelled the murders of the governmental officers, the rebels continued to threaten with death those who had opposed the rebellion. Even after the jail at La Cañada was filled with prisoners, the rebels condemned to jail yet more men. Captain José Caballero wrote of the terror of the people caused by this "most disastrous revolution, scattering confusion among the inhabitants, disclaiming all the laws and constitution and committing extravagant errors in their place, leaving us in a miserable state of barbarism." The rebels, wrote Caballero, "convoked an assembly to choose two commissioners to give account to the Supreme Government protesting their obedience, a reasonable action, but then without respecting even the government they themselves had set up, they constantly put new and alarming schemes into practice . . ." What Caballero did not realize was that there were now two rebel factions—the reasonable, headed by Gonzales, and the alarming, still agitating in Río Arriba.[73]

Rebellion at Taos

About September 3, Padre Martínez arrived breathless from Taos. He brought news that on September 2, villagers and Pueblo Indians had assembled hastily in the streets of Taos in order to attack him and others who had not expressed their disapproval of the Pérez regime. The priest and his brother, Subprefect Santiago Martínez, fled to Santa Fe, pursued all the way by men they were convinced meant to kill them. Two days later the priest received word that the mob at Taos would receive him well. Padre Martínez returned to Taos on September 4, accompanied by Governor Gonzales and Secretary Donaciano Vigil.[74]

The governor's mission at Taos was to pacify the rebels of his native town. To serve as interim governor at Santa Fe in his absence, he appointed First Alcalde José Francisco Ortiz y Delgado. Governor Gonzales remained in Taos at least four days; Donaciano Vigil wrote a letter for him dated Taos, September 8, to the commander, Ronquillo (who probably never saw the letter, having already left Santa Fe for the safety of El Paso del Norte.)[75]

At Taos Padre Martínez was received kindly at first. Then he was forced by the Taos councilmen and armed men to sign a paper saying that he would give up the collection of church funds, perform sacraments without the usual fees, and allow the dead to be buried in the church. In signing the paper he committed all other priests in the Department to do the same. To his horror, the rebels buried one corpse in the Ranchos de Taos church, at the very steps of the chancel. Such was the news Padre Martínez wrote to his bishop at Durango, enclosing letters written by two other priests attesting to rebel insults and violence toward the Church.[76]

News brought by Padre Martínez of the fresh rebellion at Taos swept like fire through Santa Fe and Río Abajo. Soon afterwards the rebels issued an edict in the name of the governor and of the Cantón, threatening bloodshed and pillage in the capital and Río Abajo. No copy of this edict has been found, but a proclamation of Captain José Caballero to the alcaldes of Río Abajo, dated September 9, refers to rebels "now advancing to sack the capital and Río Abajo." The direct threat of violence to Santa Fe and Río Abajo forced the citizens into immediate action, and leaders rose among them to challenge the rebels.[77]

Rebels Challenged

After Governor Gonzales had left Santa Fe for Taos on September 4, the people of Santa Fe felt great relief and hope, and they immediately began to mobilize against a new invasion of their capital. The presidial troop, which had been disbanded by Pérez, voluntarily organized into a company under Captain José Caballero, to serve without pay. The officers demanded arms of Lieutenant Colonel Ronquillo, who strongly objected. On September 5 Ronquillo resigned as commander, "because the soldiers are delivered to suffering and abandonment, and I am reduced to nothing," but for a day or so he kept his other position of adjutant inspector. On September 6 the officers of the troop formed a military junta consisting of Lieutenants José Silva and José Fernández, Alfereces Francisco Martínez, Manual Ramírez, Rafael Tapia and Ramón Baca, Sergeants Baltasar Sandoval, Francisco

Campo and Antonio Sena. The officers wrote a statement denouncing the "lack of measures that Señor Ronquillo has taken to prevent the many evils that we have been suffering since August 8 last, and expect to suffer because of the improper separation he made from his office." The junta demoted Ronquillo and ordered that a letter describing its proceedings be sent to the Supreme Government by the next mail.[78]

On September 7 Ronquillo left Santa Fe, with "indications of fear and cowardice," as Manuel Armijo wrote later. José Caballero then became principal commander, to the joy of Subcomisario Francisco Baca y Terrus, who wrote that Caballero's new position would restore "the security and quiet that has disappeared in our land." Now, with Gonzales and Donaciano Vigil in Taos and Ronquillo on the road to El Paso del Norte, the rebel government lacked representation in the capital of Santa Fe, and its enemies worked rapidly to undermine it.[79]

Vicente Sánchez Vergara was the leader of the governor's enemies in Santa Fe. Under his direction the citizens of the city came forward with provisions, goods, and arms to sustain the troop—barrels of gunpowder donated by José (Jesse) Sutton, a pound of lead from Sánchez Vergara himself, 254 sheep and fifty fanegas of wheat from Juan Estevan Pino, three pounds of gunpowder from Francisco Sarracino, four pieces of cloth from Juan Rafael Ortiz, and a gift of pesos from the United States commercial agent, Manuel Álvarez. Sánchez Vergara also sent messages to Río Abajo, keeping that district informed about such matters as the continued absence of José Gonzales from the capital and the reorganization of the presidial troop.[80]

On September 9 Commander José Caballero issued a proclamation to the alcaldes of Río Abajo, a part of which follows:

Compatriots, it is time to stop this evil; we must reestablish order at all costs. Seeing our weakness, the Navajos will continue with the Pueblos to wage war on us. The veteran company has voluntarily reorganized with arms and have sworn every one to sustain tranquillity or die in defense of the laws. The citizenry all breathe enthusiasm and decision for their sacred cause. I have ordered a force of six hundred men of Santa Fe to join with the Río Abajo people at Bernalillo where they will be led by whomever you think to elect commander in chief.[81]

With this proclamation, Commander Caballero challenged Río Abajo to produce men and a leader to reinforce Santa Fe's presidial company and its army of six hundred citizens.

Río Abajo Mobilizes

One of the citizens of Río Abajo who kept Vicente Sánchez Vergara informed was the priest of Tomé, Francisco Ignacio de Madariaga. Curate Madariaga was a man of action: Manuel Armijo later gave him credit for conceiving the idea of an opposition army and of "raising the glorious cry of order and laws when no one dared to breathe and when it seemed foolhardy even to imagine it."[82]

Madariaga invited a number of the leading men of Bernalillo and Valencia counties to meet with him at the village of Tomé on September 8. The meeting was very brief; the impulsive rico Mariano Chávez immediately rose and proposed that an army be formed,

"sufficiently strong for every purpose that the occasion demands. It ought to be under the command of some person abundantly able to lead it to certain victory, a victory that will carry with

itself into the ranks of the insurgents such a degree of consternation and fear as will forever quiet this bloody uprising . . . I know
of no one better qualified to lead our army than General Manuel
Armijo; therefore I ask this assemblage to declare him to be our
leader." No other name was presented to the people for their
consideration. All seemed to acquiesce in the selection of Don
Manuel as their commander.[83]

So reads Francisco Perea's account, but Perea was only
eight years old in 1837, and his account contains errors:
"General" Armijo was not then a general, but only a lieutenant in the Albuquerque militia, and he took command
of the army only after others had declined it, according to
his service record of 1841:

In the year 1837 a part of the department rebelled against the
constitutional laws that made it a department, and on the 8th of
September a proclamation pronounced for order at Tomé. A force
of seven hundred men was gathered from all the sane people who
adhered to this plan, and after offering command of the forces to
the principal men, none wished to accept it because of the difficulty and danger involved, and in consequence, the same force
unanimously proclaimed him [Armijo] as its chief, naming him
colonel and commander in chief of the liberating army, which he
accepted for the good of the country, commanding it until the
capital of Santa Fe was occupied.[84]

On September 8, 1837, the assembly at Tomé drew up a
pronouncement later known as the Plan of Tomé. Its authors
called themselves "citizens who love their country and favor
the constitution and the laws, and who fear the anarchy and
abuse of property threatened by the Cantón of La Cañada."
To assure the government of the obedience of the district of

Albuquerque, the assembly agreed on ten articles, an extract of which follows:

1) The sole recognized authority will be the prefect of Albuquerque [Antonio Sandoval] who is the only legitimate authority still alive.

2) No one will be deprived of property or rights.

3) An armed force will be raised with Manuel Armijo as commander, Mariano Chávez as second in command, and Vicente Sánchez Vergara as secretary.

4) If another commander should later be named, he will continue the same actions as have already been taken.

5) The Pueblo Indians should not be involved or take sides until the Supreme Government names a government, and will in the meantime govern themselves.

6) The Pueblos will be informed of this by three Isleta natives who have been taught these articles.

7) The authority of the *Cantón* is disavowed.

8) The commander of the liberating forces will raise money for his army and religiously reimburse owners for anything commandeered.

9) An *extraordinario violento* will be sent to inform authorities in Chihuahua and Mexico.

10) Any contribution made by natives to the commissioners named in Santa Fe will be religiously repaid.[85]

The Plan was signed by Manuel Armijo, Francisco Ignacio de Madariaga, José Salazar, Pablo Salazar, Alcalde José Francisco Montoya, Miguel Olona, Juan de Madariaga, and Alcalde Manuel Antonio Armijo. In Santa Fe the pronouncement and election of Manuel Armijo was received with "heartfelt cheering and acclamations." Captain Caballero's six hundred men immediately left Santa Fe and marched to Bernalillo, where Armijo had established his camp and had begun recruiting men and collecting supplies, begging the people for arms, food, and forage for his army. [86]

Commander Manuel Armijo

On September 12, as Armijo was about to leave Bernalillo for Santa Fe with his troops, he wrote a letter to the minister of war, reporting the course of events up to this time (document 4). The letter was published in the *Diario del Gobierno*, on October 19. After several grandiloquent paragraphs by the editor, deploring the "barbarous and execrable revolution that has bloodied New Mexico," the letter marches forward in Armijo's more vigorous style to describe what happened: Governor Pérez confronted the rebels with a very small force, composed mostly of Pueblo Indians from Cochití, Santo Domingo, and Sandía; the Indians first deserted and then attacked him; the governor and his companions were killed on the road to Santo Domingo after making a brave defense; an army has been formed with Armijo in command, to bring to order the many unhappy people deceived by the rebels, and to punish their leaders; New Mexico has men capable of committing such horrors, but also honorable, faithful men who did not hesitate to speak up against them on September 8; and finally, help has been sought from the commanding general at Chihuahua, who was informed immediately of all that occurred. [87]

On September 11 Governor Gonzales returned to Santa Fe from Río Arriba, "as if fleeing from the Cantón," in the words of the author of "An Account of the Chimayó Rebellion." Hardly had Gonzales dismounted from his mule and entered the secretary's office when the first alcalde of Santa Fe told him of the Plan of Tomé and ordered him to surrender, since his government was suspended. With "greatest enthusiasm" Governor Gonzales embraced and adopted the Plan in all its parts, promising to obey the laws and authorities that the Plan designated and vowing to serve until the last soldier fell—so certified the first and second alcaldes of Santa Fe in two documents, both signed with Governor Gonzales's name and rubric. Gonzales's name seems to have been written in the distinctive hand of Vicente Sánchez Vergara. The rubric following the name was crude, simple, and consistent, and was probably made by the illiterate governor himself. [88]

Perhaps the governor's enthusiasm for the Plan of Tomé was as genuine as his rubric. Perhaps he contrasted the Plan of Tomé favorably with the violent and lawless actions of the Taos and La Cañada rebels, the Cantón from which he may well have been fleeing. On the other hand, his acceptance of the Tomé plan may not have been as spontaneous and enthusiastic as the alcaldes certified, for when Manuel Armijo arrived the next day with his army, he found José Gonzales a prisoner in the Santa Fe jail. [89]

The Taos Faction

Armijo arrived at Santa Fe with his army on September 14. He was followed in weeks to come by several families with household goods, who were afraid to remain in Río Abajo after most of the armed, able-bodied men had left the region with Armijo. On the day of his arrival, Armijo met at the Governor's Palace with the officers of the Santa Fe presidial troop, to discuss steps already taken for restoring order. He proposed to the officers that if they wished to choose another commander or a different mode of procedure, they should do so. The officers unanimously agreed with the action already taken and unanimously recognized Armijo as their colonel and Mariano Chávez as their lieutenant colonel.[90]

Armijo now commanded a little over a thousand men, "all breathing enthusiasm and decision for their sacred cause," as he reported. Armijo's men were among the most respectable in Río Abajo, and they behaved with discipline, to the delight of the citizens of Santa Fe, who showed them great consideration. Most of these volunteer soldiers were unschooled in the handling of arms; Armijo's first task was to have them trained. Then he saw to the mounting of artillery, repair of arms, and procurement of ammunition. He ordered the alcalde to seize three big wagons to carry provisions for the army, with the understanding that the cost of them would be repaid "religiously" by the presidial troop. He also raised the necessary funds to maintain the troop, obtaining loans totaling 410 pesos from the foreign merchants José (Jesse) Sutton, Manuel Álvarez, John Scolly, Luis and Antonio Robidoux, and David Waldo. Río Abajo ricos contributed far more—Mariano Chávez alone gave 610 pesos, Antonio Sandoval gave 520 pesos, and others gave similar amounts.[91]

Reports reached Santa Fe that three thousand rebels were approaching the city and taking a favorable battle position—an army that must have included most of the adult males of Río Arriba. Armijo wrote Colonel Juan Estevan Pino, asking him to command the "liberating army," but Pino declined Armijo's request on September 19, pleading advanced age and frequent illness. Armijo continued in command, although it was not a position he favored, then or later. Several times in the years to come, he would protest that he was not a trained soldier and knew nothing of battle tactics, and he would beg to be relieved of command in order to serve under an experienced general. His disinclination to command troops in battle was obvious on several notorious

55

future occasions, and for this he acquired the reputation of coward.[92]

The Taos faction of the Cantón was led by Pablo Montoya, former alcalde of Taos and lieutenant colonel of the Taos militia. Montoya had a record of trouble-making; Donaciano Vigil called him a "mischievous fool" and a "brigand." Ten years later, Montoya was hung by American soldiers for fomenting the massacre of foreigners at Taos, in 1847.[93]

Armijo described the events that followed in a letter to the Supreme Government, dated October 11, 1837 (document 8). The Cantón under Pablo Montoya stopped a league and a half north of Santa Fe. Armijo's army remained in the city, while Armijo conducted a correspondence with Montoya. Armijo wrote that he meant to avoid battle and bloodshed if possible, for he knew that most of the rebels had joined the force out of ignorance or fear. He persuaded Pablo Montoya to send a letter to José Gonzales giving the "factitious causes" of the uprising; then he invited Montoya to join in a verbal treaty. Montoya came to the city with Río Arriba councilmen and alternates. Together with Armijo they drafted terms of agreement, whereby the rebels would dissolve their Cantón and recognize Armijo as both political and military head, until the president of the Republic made a decision. After various difficulties and debates, the rebels agreed to Armijo's terms, including surrender of four of the instigators of the first rebellion, who were to be indicted. The treaty was signed in Santa Fe on September 21, 1837.[94]

Why did the rebels retreat despite their great advantage in numbers? The author of "An Account of the Chimayó Rebellion" attributes the reason to lack of unity, regulation, and direction, "as always happens when a bad cause is defended." But he also cites Armijo's wisdom and tact:

Señor Armijo was informed of the state of that force which although numerous was weak because of the element that composed it, and, certain of conquering it, he used policy to avoid the effusion of blood among brother of the same country, and so wise were his measures that he succeeded without shedding a drop of blood.[95]

The rebels probably lacked guns and ammunition; they certainly lacked leadership and organization and the kind of discipline their opponents had learned from the presidial troop in their week of training in Santa Fe. Armijo may have persuaded them that not only could his forces defeat them but also that his administrative experience could serve them well in forwarding their complaints to the government and in running the department until the Supreme Government appointed a governor. It must be remembered that until now Armijo had not been considered an enemy to the rebels; he had been proposed as their deputy at one point during the junta popular, he was a native of New Mexico, and he was a former governor and well known to them. So they allowed him to persuade them to disband.

Thus concluded the revolution, wrote Armijo on October 11, with its terrifying army committing outrageous crimes. His report told of rebels inviting the wild tribes surrounding the department to form an allegiance against the government and to cut off communication with the interior of the Republic, and of rebels seducing the Pueblo Indians, a weak, credulous people addicted to the sack and spoils of war. The rebel aim, according to Armijo, was to remain independent of the Republic of Mexico and to be governed by no established law, which was their excuse for sentencing all the archives to the flames. The rebels intended to get rid of every person with even an average education and to destroy fortunes in a general sack. New Mexico would have been lost to the Republic, Armijo asserted, without the strong stand taken by some of its people at the right time, and without the support of the Supreme Government. (One might ask what support this was; Armijo did not say, nor do the records.) Armijo asked for funds to maintain three veteran companies with commanders capable of keeping discipline, and for two hundred guns to be sent immediately, to prevent another revolution. Armijo ends his report with full, generous, and individual acknowledgment of those "who promoted the pronouncement of Tomé and worked constantly without sparing personal means or sacrifice."[96]

After the treaty was signed, there was limited amnesty. Pablo Montoya and his forces retreatd to their homes, and José Gonzales was released from the Santa Fe jail to return to Taos. But the four natives of La Cañada who had begun the revolution in August were jailed in Santa Fe, according to the terms of the treaty, "in order to receive the punishment imposed by law for their enormous crime," as Armijo reported. Ten years later Donaciano Vigil wrote of Pablo Montoya's responsibility for the fate of these unhappy men and of Montoya's involvement since the beginning of the Cantón:

Destitute of any sense of shame, he brought his followers to this capital, entered into an arrangement, deserted, as a reward for their fidelity, the unfortunate Montoyas, Esquibal [sic] and Chopón, whose fate you know, and retired, himself well paid for his exploits, to his den at Taos. The whole population let the weight of their execration fall on others, and this brigand they left living on his wits—for he has no home, or known property . . . In the year 1837 this mischievous fool took as a motto for his perversity, the word Cantón . . .[97]

Governor Manuel Armijo

Manuel Armijo now assumed the governorship, with the obligation of putting the shattered government back together and reassuring the terrified populace. As an experienced administrator and as a native son who knew his people, no one was better qualified than he. Raised in a rico family of Albuquerque, he grew up handsome, bright, and arrogant, and he married the belle of New Mexico. In 1827, at the age of thirty-four, he became governor of New Mexico, a position he resigned in 1829. Then he made a fortune taking sheep and goods to sell in the interior of Mexico. In 1836 he was appointed subcomisario of New Mexico under Governor Albino Pérez. As subcomisario he was a failure, for reasons already discussed, and a month before the rebellion he was replaced by Francisco Sarracino.[98]

Armijo was hated by Americans and received very bad publicity in the United States, especially from three American writers. In his first term as governor, Armijo had confronted and arrested American smugglers among the traders from Missouri. In 1844 Josiah Gregg, a Santa Fe trader, published his influential description of New Mexico and the Santa Fe trade, *Commerce of the Prairies,* which described some of the confrontations between Armijo and the Americans. Gregg wrote nothing good about Armijo, viewing him as an "ambitious and turbulent demagogue." A second book damaging to Armijo was written by George Kendall. In his second term, Armijo captured the invading Texans and sent them to Mexico on foot. Among them was Kendall, editor of the *New Orleans Picayune*. In 1842 Kendall published sketches about the Texan expedition to Santa Fe in his newspaper, accusing Armijo of "assassinations, robberies, violent debauchery, extortions, and innumerable acts of broken faith." In 1844 Kendall's sketches appeared in a best-selling book, *Narrative of the Texan Santa Fe Expedition*. A third account was that of W. H. H. Davis, United States circuit attorney and territorial secretary of New Mexico from 1853 to 1857, who wrote a book entitled *El Gringo; or, New Mexico and Her People*. Davis's book was based partly on the accounts of Kendall and Gregg and partly on other New Mexican material, including public documents that Davis reputedly carried away with him when he was removed from office on charges of embezzlement. All three books make delightful reading, and Armijo's reputation is still suffering from their popularity.[99]

It has often been written by followers of Kendall and Gregg that Manuel Armijo secretly fomented the rebellion of 1837. Kendall wrote that after Armijo was deposed from his customs-house job, he secretly plotted revolt among the Pueblo Indians assembled at La Cañada, and having raised this whirlwind, directed the storm to his own advantage. W. H. H. Davis wrote that Armijo and his fellow conspirators Juan Estevan Pino and Juan Rafael Ortiz dispatched secret agents all over New Mexico to excite rebellion and to regain for Armijo the office of subcomisario, which he much desired. If in fact Armijo raised a whirlwind, it was probably not to regain the job of subcomisario. Near the end of his ineffective term in this position, he wrote Governor Pérez that "according to what I have heard, I am going to have to be comisario in this department forever, because of not being able to find somebody else." Kendall also asserted that when the rebels camped in Santa Fe, on August 10, Armijo left his hacienda at Albuquerque and appeared at the camp to claim the governorship, but that the rebels ignored his claim because he had not taken part in the battle. Although Gregg repeats the story in many of Kendall's words, he writes that he heard it from Armijo's own brother. [100]

There are reasons to doubt that Armijo hurried up from Albuquerque to claim the governorship. Common sense might question that a man whom Kendall and Gregg both characterized as a coward, would have the courage (or the time) to ride fifty miles between Albuquerque and Santa Fe to present himself at a camp of frenzied rebels, even assuming, as Kendall did, that Armijo might have been in league with some of the leaders. Donaciano Vigil, then secretary of the Cantón and probably present at the acclamation of José Gonzales as governor, wrote that "those who planned and furnished the means for the uprising expected that day to be chosen to office, which they had so much desired previously, and when they saw their hopes frustrated, searched for means to continue the anarchy." Vigil could hardly be referring to Manuel Armijo, whose subsequent efforts were plainly directed at ending the anarchy. [101]

Only Americans openly accused Armijo of promoting the rebellion, and not all of them at that. Manuel Álvarez, commercial agent of the United States traders, told Armijo that the foreigners in the department directed the rebellion and other uprisings. The commanding general at Chihuahua also accused the Americans of fomenting rebellion, but most Mexicans of the interior thought the Texans were responsible. Vicente Sánchez Vergara blamed the rebellion on the example of the rebellious californios in 1836, who revolted against a nonnative governor similar to Governor Pérez in his unpopular devotion to centralism and his flagrant adultery. And there were other suspects. Padre Antonio José Martínez was accused by later writers of being a conspirator, either alone or in league with Armijo and the Penitentes, as we have seen. [102]

It might be reasonable to assume, along with the American writers, that since Manuel Armijo was the beneficiary of the rebellion, he was also its instigator. However, no evidence of Armijo's complicity in the rebellion exists outside the accusation of Gregg, Kendall, and Davis frequently repeated through the years. Given the irritation of the people of Río Arriba in 1837 and the incidents that fanned it into flames of fury, probably no "conspiracy" of outsiders was necessary to incite rebellion.

Armijo's first action as governor was to establish his right to govern, which he recognized as outside the law. His circular of September 24 to the alcaldes of Río Arriba begins, "On commencing to exercise the powers of superior political and military chief of this territory, in which necessity and not law has placed me . . ." The circular then reviews the bases of Armijo's assumption of power: his appointment on September 8 as commander of the liberating army, with the rank of colonel; his formal recognition by the presidial troop as colonel and chief of the liberating army; and the acknowledgement by the rebels that he was military and political chief, "which I could not refuse without failing in the duty of a citizen." His ambition, he writes, was only to destroy the insurrection of La Cañada and keep men under arms until orders from the Supreme Government arrived. While awaiting these orders, Armijo writes, he will maintain quiet, observation of the laws, obedience to authority, and the indispensable order which is the life of every society, even if he has to use severe measures. [103]

Armijo's American critics seized upon his assumption of power as usurpation. In Kendall's ironic words:

The ambitious tyrant, now that his enemies were either murdered or dispersed, reigned supreme in New Mexico. One of his first steps was to bribe the army to proclaim him governor and commander in chief; his next, to send off a highly-colored account of his own exploits in favor of Federalism to the city of Mexico, and no officer can more adroitly adopt the high-sounding fanfaronade style in wording a dispatch or an address than Manuel Armijo. Such disinterested patriotism, such love of the confederacy, and such daring bravery as he had manifested could not go unrewarded, and a return of post from Mexico brought documents confirming him in his station of governor, with the additional title of colonel of cavalry.[104]

Gregg's book concurs entirely with Kendall's, even to the adoption of Kendall's phrases: "After his triumphal entrance into the capital, Armijo caused himself to be proclaimed Governor and Commandante General, and immediately dispatched couriers to Mexico with a highly colored account of his own exploits, which procured him a confirmation of those titles." W. H. H. Davis has the same story, although in different words.[105]

Manuel Armijo was not a man to minimize his triumphs; nevertheless, his letter of September 12, 1837, was a straightforward narrative of the disaster and could not in any way be described as a "highly colored account of his own exploits." Nor did it later obtain for him the appointment of governor. President Bustamante had appointed Armijo governor on September 12, the very day Armijo wrote that letter, and also the very day the *Diario del Gobierno* published the first news of the rebellion in Mexico City. This was a month before the government could have known of Armijo's negotiations with the Taos faction and his assumption of the governorship. The government plainly believed, on the basis of Armijo's record as former governor (and not, of course, on his sorry record as subcomisario) that he was the strongest candidate to fill the vacancy left by Pérez's death.[106]

Along with certain skeptical Americans cited above, some of Armijo's fellow countrymen doubtless suspected that Armijo's assumption of the governorship was not inspired by pure patriotism. Armijo himself seems to have known that his motives were questioned. In a circular of October 5 to his people, he emphasizes that the position of governor which he "unfortunately" held was an "enormous personal responsibility" and a "delicate and painful burden." He further remarks that he does not need the salary, and that he does not fear that his motives are suspect—a strong hint that indeed he did fear it![107]

Rebels at Truchas

Long before he knew of his appointment as governor, Armijo exercised the full powers of chief executive to maintain order, and he threatened to use some of the "severe measures" he had warned of in his circular of September 24 to the alcaldes. On October 5 he issued another circular to the alcaldes, saying that he expected soon to give up command of the troops to a commander chosen by the military chief in Chihuahua. Because the revolution of La Cañada was still in a dangerous and fluctuating state, he expected this circular to serve as a final warning to every alcalde to report any suspicious movements or be judged a traitor.[108]

On October 17 Armijo returned to his home, probably because of the severe pain in his leg from an old wound that regularly sent him from the high-altitude chill of Santa Fe to the warmer climate of Albuquerque. While he was away, the Governor's Palace was being renovated for occupancy after its possession by the rebels. In Armijo's absence Captain José Caballero was left in charge of the troop, with orders from Armijo that the four prisoners—the two Montoyas, Esquibel, and Vigil—should be beheaded if there were new disorders in Río Arriba. [109]

As Armijo had warned, the revolution was not over. At 6:30 on the morning of October 18, a messenger from the alcalde of Santa Cruz arrived at Santa Fe with news of rebel factions whipping up an uprising in the mountain village of Las Truchas. The next day Captain Caballero prepared to send fifty men under Lieutenant José Hernández to La Cañada and Las Truchas. On the same day Caballero received another letter from the alcalde of La Cañada, advising that the insurgents of Las Truchas intended to divide their forces and invade Santa Fe from different directions. Alarmed, Caballero suspended the march of Lieutenant Hernández and his men, fearing for the safety of the capital. It was suspected that three or four individuals from Santa Fe were in communication with the rebels of Río Arriba and would presumably inform them if the departure of the presidial troop left the city undefended. [110]

At Albuquerque Armijo was immediately informed of the Truchas rebellion. On October 19 he wrote Colonel Juan Estevan Pino, asking once more that Pino come up from his Hacienda de Galisteo to lead troops against the rebel forces. Pino answered as before, that illness prevented him. On the same day, Armijo wrote Caballero, ordering that the four hostages be decapitated. [111]

Caballero wrote back that he had doubts about the timing of such an execution and about its effect on the populace. He called a junta of his officers to read carefully all the orders and letters pertaining to the case. Devising a clever compromise to delay the sentence, the officers unanimously resolved that the order of the commanding general should be obeyed, but that the Santa Fe plaza should be filled with soldiers to put down any resistance to the execution of the hostages, and that at the moment the rebels attempted to attack the plaza, the hostages would be beheaded. The document was signed by the principal military and civil officers then in Santa Fe.[112]

Armijo received notice of the officers' decision on October 23. Furious, he wrote Caballero that however slight the possibility that the revolution at Truchas would spread, the troops had disobeyed his express orders, which should have been carried out for the sake of discipline. But he would overlook the disobedience and send the active militia of Albuquerque under Alférez Julián Armijo for the protection of Santa Fe. As it turned out, the rebels at Truchas never attacked Santa Fe, and the leaders of the first revolt, languishing in the Santa Fe jail, retained their heads for a while longer.[113]

The presidial troops that had assembled so spiritedly in September to defend Santa Fe were hungry and rebellious by November. They had received no pay, nor was there any money in the treasury to pay them or the civil servants. Although Armijo had said in his letter of October 11 that the counterrevolution would not have succeeded without the "protecting hand" of the Supreme Government, records show no help at all from that source until January. On November 4 Treasurer Juan Rafael Ortiz wrote Armijo in Albuquerque that he had offered the soldiers wheat at the stiff price of four pesos per fanega in lieu of their salaries. At first the soldiers objected violently and threatened to revolt, but finally they agreed to take it at that price.[114]

A soldier's revolt at this perilous time was to be avoided

at all costs; Armijo returned from Albuquerque, and he and Juan Rafael spent the rest of 1837 raising money and supplies for the presidial troop. Good citizens of the department gave generously in cash or kind, until by December 31 nearly five thousand pesos had been raised to maintain the men.[115]

Federal Troops

While still at Albuquerque, on October 27 Armijo had written General Jose J. Calvo at Chihuahua about the "disagreeable turn the revolution has taken" and had asked for help. In answer General Calvo wrote on November 15 that a squadron of Veracruz dragoons of Zacatecas under Captain Tomás Zuloaga would leave the next day from Chihuahua with fifty artillerymen, two mortars, and corresponding weapons, along with remount, uniforms, and funds. General Calvo himself would follow with the rest of his command of ninety-four men, marching on the double to El Paso del Norte (about 330 miles away). Calvo's troops apparently joined those under Zuloaga at El Paso, and on December 11 the combined force under Lieutenant Colonel Cayetano Justiniani, commander at El Paso, began the 250-mile march to Santa Fe.[116]

Armijo expected the troops to arrive the first week in January, and to consist of a section of the vanguard under Justiniani, with more forces close behind, under General Calvo and General Mariano Arista. But the generals and their troops never arrived. On January 9, 1838, the first section of federal troops under Justiniani reached Santa Fe from El Paso del Norte—94 dragoons of the Veracruz squadron (9 of whom promptly deserted), 12 artillerymen of the Chihuahua Artillery, 22 men of the San Buenaventura squadron,

26 from San Eleazario, and 25 from El Paso del Norte, totaling 167 trained and well-supplied troops.[117]

Justiniani brought with him the long-awaited decision of the Supreme Government, in the form of Armijo's appointments as constitutional governor, principal commandant, and colonel of militia. Then Armijo issued a proclamation to the people as "Constitutional Governor and Principal Commandant," reporting his appointments. Most of the proclamation is a diatribe against the rebels, in what Kendall called Armijo's "high-sounding fanfaronade style," greatly admired by his fellow countrymen; but there is some substance beneath the steamy verbiage. Armijo describes the Pueblos as innocent victims of "ambitious and unnatural types," whose heads will be cut off by the "knife of the law," a metaphor revealing that his mind was still occupied with the decapitation of the hostages—but not without due process, for he also refers to an impending investigation of "those perverted criminals."[118]

The arrival of the Veracruz squadron caused difficulties with the people and soldiers of Santa Fe. On January 12 Armijo issued a proclamation ordering the citizens not to quarrel with the new soldiers nor to raise prices in their stores, but to take all complaints to the proper authority. Citizens were not to create disturbances by frequenting wineshops and gambling establishments with soldiers, nor should they receive pledges of soldiers' guns, horses, or ammunition.[119]

More Days of Disorder

The new soldiers did not have long to wait before their services were required. On January 19 Armijo learned that early in January Antonio Vigil ("El Coyote") had issued a maundering and ill-written circular from Las Truchas to participants in the La Cañada reunión from the Taos Valley towns of "San Francisco del Rancho de Taos, Río Chiquito, Pueblo de Taos, Arroyo Seco, Plaza de San Antonio Desmontes y Ranchito," calling upon them to march at once. Antonio Vigil's circular recalled that a departmental law had been published in 1837 and that those who "unsheathed the sword in defense of this law" had been put to death. Don José Gonzales had been chosen defender of the laws by "harmonious vote from the bosom of this peaceful territory," but now Señor Armijo had usurped that position, not by a vote of the people, but by violence and force and by imprisoning the four defenders of the Santa Cruz pronouncement. Wherever this circular is published, wrote Antonio Vigil, let the cry be raised, "Long Live God, and the country, and the faith of Jesus Christ, and Antonio Vigil!" Once more the people cried out for the right to choose their own rulers, but feebly and ungrammatically. [120]

The purpose of this naive document was apparently to raise a force to free the hostages. When it came to Armijo's attention, he issued another circular to the people, dated January 19, containing a stern warning to the Pueblo Indians to stay out of the coming fight. On January 22 the juez of Cochití Pueblo sent Armijo news of a meeting of Cochití Indians with the rebels of La Cañada. Armijo immediately wrote a letter addressed to "the commander of the reunión of La Cañada," asking what his motives and intentions were, and ordering him to dissolve his reunión immediately and send his supporters to their homes. The rebel commander was ordered also to present José Gonzales and Antonio Vigil to Armijo at the capital. If the rebels were obedient to this order they would be pardoned, but if not, the first to die would be the Montoyas, Vigil, and Esquibel, now in the

Santa Fe jail. Armijo gave the commander of the reunión twenty-four hours to reply.[121]

Antonio Vigil replied, but his answer is not in the archives; whatever it was, Armijo did not find it satisfactory. On January 23 Armijo sent copies of it to the military commander and to the alcaldes of Ábiquiu and Ojo Caliente, along with a letter saying that Vigil was again leading a revolution and asking the alcaldes to support the laws as their jurisdictions had always done and to warn their people not to take part in rebel schemes. Then Armijo prepared to carry out the terms of his ultimatum.[122]

Execution of the Prisoners

At nine o'clock on the morning of January 24, Juan José Esquibel, Juan Vigil, Desiderio Montoya, and his brother Antonio Abad Montoya were decapitated, as Armijo wrote in a circular of that date. He said the criminals were in the process of being judged under formulas and covenants of law, but that when Antonio Vigil and his new rebels threatened to rescue them by force, they were executed.[123]

The prisoners were executed near the Garita, a small, decaying colonial fortification on the east side of the main road entering the city from the north. W. H. H. Davis wrote in 1853 that the hostages and José Gonzales were subject to court-martial and sentenced to death, along with "many of the persons who had aided him [Armijo] with money and arms, and had been instrumental in placing him at the head of affairs . . . and Armijo is said to have caused many others to be privately assassinated." Many citizens tried to get a remittance of the sentence, wrote Davis, but even though Armijo was much censured for his cruelty, he was deaf to every appeal on behalf of his former confederates and asserted that since the court had found them guilty, he had no authority to pardon them.[124]

No records of the trial or court-martial mentioned by Armijo and W. H. H. Davis remain in the New Mexico archives, nor is there any evidence that other men were either sentenced to death by the court or privately assassinated by Armijo, as Davis suggests. Davis may have based his conclusions on Kendall's statement that Armijo ordered the deaths of José Gonzales and the four rebels in order to hide his connection with them and that he committed other unspecified assassinations.[125]

Despite the Americans' horror at the Mexican style of executing prisoners, Armijo was well within legal and traditional bounds in this action. In fact the historian George Lockhart Rives gives ample evidence that during the Mexican period and afterwards, prisoners were executed regularly in order to suppress rebellion. Hardly a year before the Río Arriba rebellion, General Santa Anna had ordered the execution of 350 Texan prisoners near Goliad, a massacre that Rives shows to be supported by Mexican law and precedent. If indeed there were citizens who tried to gain a reprieve for Armijo's prisoners, others were doubtless surprised that Armijo would order a court-martial to determine the guilt of these obviously subversive men.[126]

Armijo's order of January 24 to execute the prisoners by decapitation was carried out that very day. Nevertheless, two young boys, brought to the execution for the moral lesson, describe the death of the prisoners by firing squad. These children did not publish accounts of the execution until fifty years later, however, and their accounts are full of errors in other matters.[127]

Battle at Pojoaque

On January 27 Armijo marched with his forces toward Santa Cruz de la Cañada for a battle with the rebels. Armijo's forces totaled 582 men, including Veracruz dragoons under the command of Lieutenant Colonel Justiniani, an energetic and skillful commander. Justiniani courteously ceded command to Armijo, although Armijo was junior to him in rank, but it was Justiniani who directed the movements of the troops. Thirteen hundred rebels had situated themselves to the best advantage in the *puerto* or *puertocito* ("pass," or "outpost") of Pojoaque, about seventeen miles north of Santa Fe. The morning was cruelly cold and snow lay on the ground, making the rebel strongholds on top of crags and hills nearly inaccessible to the attacking soldiers. From these heights, large groups of rebels fired down on the soldiers, attempting to flank them. Justiniani sent the Veracruz squadron to the front and used the rest of the men in pickets and guerrilla bands to put the enemy to flight. Within a quarter of an hour the soldiers had taken the field and sent the rebels fleeing north toward Santa Cruz. Twenty rebels were killed, eight were captured, and many more were wounded. In a second action, later that day, rebels who had entrenched themselves at the top of a high, forested point of land loosed their gunfire on the soldiers below. The troops fired back, dislodging the snipers from their ambuscade and scattering them, and Armijo entered Santa Cruz without opposition. The Veracruz squadron suffered four men dead and others wounded. [128]

The above account of the battle is based on letters of Manuel Armijo to his friend Carlos María Bustamante, the famous Mexican journalist and historian. American descriptions of the battle differ both in substance and in bias. Kendall writes that José Gonzales had rallied around him a mob that Armijo routed with heavy reinforcements from the south, putting Gonzales and four of his chief officers to death, "more to prevent disclosures than for any crime they had committed." Gregg adds a much-quoted little story of the battle:

It appeared that, when the army arrived within view of the insurgent force, Armijo evinced the greatest perturbation. In fact, he was upon the point of retiring without venturing an attack, when Captain Munoz of the Vera Cruz dragoons, exclaimed, "What's to be done, General Armijo? If your excellency will but permit me, I will oust that rabble in an instant with my little company alone." Armijo, having given his consent, the gallant captain rushed upon the insurgents who yielded at once, and fled precipitately—suffering a loss of about a dozen men, among whom was the deposed Governor Gonzales, who, having been caught in the town after the skirmish had ended, was instantly shot, without the least form of trial. [129]

The American accounts are no more biased than the traditional accounts of natives of New Mexico, whose hatred of the rebels was so strong that they would not ascribe to them even the courage of defending their positions at Pojoaque. Rafael Chacón writes that when Armijo placed his troops in battle line and ordered a cannon to be fired, Captain Muñoz adjusted his cap, drew his sword, and shouted "Forward, Veracruz!" and as he charged, the rebels ran away in great disorder and scattered all over the countryside. Pedro Sánchez recites the tradition that when the rebel San Juan Indian Rafaelito fired the first shot, killing Chiquito Alarid, Armijo instantly yelled "Forward! to death or to victory!" The rebels turned and fled over the hills, not stopping until they reached Arroyo Seco, fifteen miles north. Antonio Vigil was killed in this action, says Sánchez, and his body was hung from a post at the crossroads of Jacona and Pojoaque as a warning to rebels.[130]

According to Pedro Sánchez, who inherited the stories of Padre Antonio José Martínez, Armijo and his troops were lodged in the parish rectory at Santa Cruz after the battle. There José Gonzales presented himself and asked for security for his town and the assurance that no taxes would be imposed. Armijo answered politely that he would consider none of Gonzales's requests and that his object was to establish peace in the shortest possible time. Turning to Padre Martínez, Armijo said, "Padre, confess this genízaro, hear his confession so that he may be given five shots." Padre Martínez did so and then turned him over to the soldiers, who shot him in the castillo of Santa Cruz.[131]

The actions of Padre Martínez as chaplain to the troops at Pojoaque were a source of great pride to himself. Writing in 1838 in the third person, Martínez boasted that he "deported himself as a brave and charitable soul hearing the confessions of the wounded with bullets whistling over his head." He added that the success of the battle was largely due to his own efforts: to information he provided the governor before the battle, and to an armed barricade he set up to keep the Taos rebels from joining their comrades at Pojoaque.[132]

The battle at Pojoaque was the last of the rebellion. Pious hands erected rude crosses beside the road, to mark the places where men fell in battle. Some rebels of La Cañada later signed representations that they repented the rebellion. The rebel leader Pablo Montoya of Taos was now on the side of order, but only to the extent that he reported war dances held at Taos Pueblo to instigate the assassination of Governor Armijo.[133]

The rebellion in Río Arriba ended not only in defeat for

the rebels and death for their leaders, but in the failure of their hope for a democratic New Mexico. Their dream of "laws analogous to the Department" was dead, their tentative ideas of independence or of union with another nation were ended. It was an overwhelming victory for the hated centralism that stole the people's right to choose their own leaders, make their own laws, impose their own taxes, and conduct their own commerce.

Or was this really the end of popular rights? Actually, through the appointment of Manuel Armijo as governor, the rebellion accomplished to some degree a few of the gains it envisaged. Not many laws beneficial to New Mexico were passed by the Mexican Congress, but in years to come, Governor Armijo managed to restore some lost liberties by simply ignoring laws he found detrimental to the department. The presidial troop, that wretched handful of ragged, hungry, and rebellious soldiers, were at first given a tough course in discipline by the governor himself and later were occasionally furnished guns and supplies through the governor's constant badgering of the Supreme Government. As the troop's morale improved, however slightly, the militia also seemed to take heart, forcing the Navajos to reduce the number of their depredations and to observe their treaties more carefully. Governor Armijo fostered foreign trade (and his own wealth and power) through low, illegal tariffs, and as the traders' confidence in his government increased, so, in some measure, did New Mexico's economic prosperity. In a few years, a little hope began to shine on the troubled province of New Mexico—not much, to be sure, but enough to prevent another rebellion like that of 1837 in Río Arriba.[134]

Part 2

Documents

Documents

Notes to documents will be found following the text of each. All translations are by Janet Lecompte.

1. True Account of the Effects Belonging to Señor Colonel Don Albino Pérez, Showing the Distribution Made of those that Could be Recovered after His Death and the Whereabouts of the Rest, as Far as Could Be Ascertained

This document is a list of the effects of Pérez that escaped José Gonzales's distribution to his partisans on August 27, 1837. The list is dated just a year later, written in Donaciano Vigil's hand, and refers to an auction of the goods, perhaps on this date, to satisfy Pérez's creditors. It gives a remarkable picture of the artifacts that surrounded Albino Pérez and of his luxurious life-style. It indicates Jesse Sutton's friendship with Pérez and his willingness to finance Pérez's extravagance—doubtless in return for some major favors. The document tells of Colonel Pérez's fancy accoutrements on campaign, his debts, and his housekeeper-mistress, called in the document "the señora who served him." The destructiveness of the mob is illustrated by the six wooden frames of sofas stripped to their calico covering (the Governor's Palace had to be renovated after the rebels had occupied it for a month) and the governor's epaulets, uniform and hat, "all very mistreated and without any value." Armijo bought a red pinto horse and Pérez's military uniform "very reasonable" in settlement of a debt Pérez had owed him.

—A two-wheeled cart (*quitrín*) with two horses that Pérez ordered to be brought from the United States by José Sutton; not having paid Sutton for it, Pérez returned it to Sutton the night he left the city; Sutton took it back only for considerations of friendship, and for the same considerations he aided Pérez with three hundred pesos in gold for his journey, despite the fact that Pérez already owed him more than two thousand pesos. This is what the accounts of the aforesaid Sutton indicate, and it is very well known that this merchant was financing Señor Pérez freely to cover his great expenses.

—Some bearskins of black fur and others of beaver; these were kept by the family that served Señor Pérez, and they were sold to different persons.

—A pair of canteens with their leather cases and a campaign tent; although these things were used by Señor Pérez, they were not his but were bought from the estate of Lieutenant Colonel Blas de Hinojos, and when the creditors of Hinojos claimed them, they were delivered to them.

—A camp bed, thought to be in possession of the señora who served him.

—Various large gilded mirrors; Don Francisco Sarracino claimed them as loans.

—A chest of drawers; claimed as a loan by the widow of Don Santiago Abreu; and a dressing table which is the property of the señora who served him.

—A large table clock; Don Juan Esteban Pino claimed it as a loan.

—Six sofas covered with calico; they were stripped by the

revolutionary mob; all that remained to be sold at the auction were the wooden frames.

—A camp chair of calfskin decorated with silver; in possession of Señor Armijo who bought it at the auction for eighty-five pesos.

—Another of the same, American, of bearskin according to report; the same señora who served Señor Pérez sold it to a foreigner who left for the United States on the same day of the catastrophe.

—A small, very light, exquisite rifle; it was the firearm that Señor Pérez had in his hand when he died; in consequence it fell into the hands of the Indians who sold it to some foreigners. Don Vicente Sánchez Vergara bought it from Doctor Henry Masure and sold it to Lieutenant Colonel José Manuel de Aponte who took it with him to Mexico.

—A double-barreled gun with its caissons, pledged to Señor Pérez for forty pesos by Don Diego Beyta of Santa Fe; but the term having expired for earning interest, it was finally auctioned off and sold.

—A red pinto horse raised by Navajos; his epaulets, uniform, and hat, all very maltreated and without any value so that they could not be sold at the auction, those in possession of Señor Armijo in payment of three hundred seventy-five pesos in silver that Señor Pérez owed him, and very reasonable.

—Another horse with white quarters taken by Rafael García in the days of disorder for a hundred pesos that Pérez had borrowed from him, and sold for goods to a trader who left for the United States; after that the goods were recovered, inventoried, and auctioned.

—Another horse of a solid dark color brought from the United States; it was in possession of Tomás Valencia in payment of a debt of two hundred fifty pesos that Señor Pérez owed him; this horse was not recovered later because it was unserviceable.

—Another of the same color also of foreign origin given by Pérez to Julian Tenorio as a gift, long before Pérez's misfortune.

—Another of the same, a Navajo roan; Señor Pérez traded it for a mule to Don José María Gutiérrez when he went on campaign.

—A large dun saddle mule in possession of Señor Don Mariano Chávez; Senor Pérez owed this individual fifteen hundred pesos in hard money loaned to him, and another large sum owed for supply of goods.

—Other mules; no one has them.

The ordinary clothes and other objects inventoried were sold judicially and the cash proceeds went to pay what Señor Pérez owed to the municipal fund of this city and to the Administrator of Mails. In said auction was sold a steel garrison sword that went to Don Juan Perea for twenty-five pesos for which Señor Armijo later gave thirty pesos and so he has possession of it.

Santa Fe August 27, 1838.

(From the Ritch Collection [RI-172], Henry E. Huntington Library, San Marino, California)

2. Address of Donaciano Vigil to the Departmental Assembly of New Mexico, June 22, 1846

Donaciano Vigil was a clever man who usually managed to land right-side up, although he was in trouble frequently in the 1830s for insubordination and blunt speaking. But he was respected in his time, and liked by the Americans (he was governor of New Mexico in 1850, when New Mexico was a

United States territory). In considering this speech before the Departmental Assembly in 1846, criticizing Pérez and defending Manuel Armijo, one must remember that Donaciano Vigil was being heard by men who knew very well what he was talking about, and who probably agreed with him.

Excellent Assembly

The nation being of a disposition to adopt a new constitution, I find this occasion opportune and very useful to New Mexico to suggest that you charge our representative with requesting of the proper authority that in future the political and military commands of this department be entrusted to persons native to it, or who at the time of their nomination have lived among us sufficient time to know our interest and the different needs peculiar to our situation.

This proposition, whose object is to assure the tranquility and security of peace, perhaps will be attributed to local pride by those who know neither our situation nor our history, but you and the observant men who have noted the vicissitudes that some administrations have caused us for lack of these requisites will firmly acquit me of such trivial motivation.

The location of our country surrounded on all sides by heathen Indians that harass us most of the time, the extreme poverty of most of our citizens (because of which no direct tax has been possible nor will it be for a long time), and the scarcity and irregularity of income that can be relied on when most urgently needed, reduces New Mexicans to a life of hardship that I believe no other department of the Republic experiences in the same degree.

Therefore it is not strange that when the Supreme Government has sent us officers for either the political or military command or both together, whose talents and services elsewhere merited confidence as being accustomed to the style and management of the interior departments where the population, education, and wealth only require making good use of the resources, these same officers arriving in our country where these elements are lacking and the deficiencies are many, are perplexed and unsuccessful in using the resources of our country, such as they are, either for peace or for war; others by not allowing for our circumstances and resenting not being able to govern us as laws and circumstances require or permit in the other departments of the Republic, have left us remembering their administrations with little gratitude.

I will explain this better by relating some fragments of our history in the last three years.

Señor Don Alvino Pérez came to New Mexico in 1835 with the highest recommendations of the Supreme Government, of the governmental periodicals, and of many other newspapers of the interior. Scarcely had he arrived at Santa Fe than he surrounded himself with the best-educated men of the country and also, as he thought, the most patriotic, and he delivered himself entirely to their counsel. With the help of these on various occasions he hoped to establish a government in New Mexico similar to the constitution and laws in force in the Republic, cutting at the root the abuses of the old colonial system and other irregularities that he observed, and the ignorance or lack of zeal of the previous governors. The people of New Mexico did not doubt the good intentions of Señor Pérez; at that time, in spite of later events, most were persuaded that if the happiness of New Mexico could have been dependent on only the good intentions and vigilance of this gentleman, he would have procured it for us. But in spite of his great aptitude, his lack of practical knowledge of the character, interests, and traditional customs of New Mexicans made him commit errors that caused us bitter days matched in our history only by the general rebellion of the Indians in the year 1694 [1690].

In the nomination of his employees he entirely neglected to consider influential men of wealth, who lacked the knowledge he thought indispensable for the undertaking, and considering themselves spurned, they soon tried to impair the reputation of Señor Pérez. His favorite employees, sure of the regard he had for them from the beginning, were abusing his confidence and in this way they were cooperating with the declared enemies of Señor Pérez in slandering his government. In the campaign that Señor Pérez made against the Navajo he succeeded in achieving important advantages, but when he tried to make peace with them, he showed that he was aware neither of the nature of the savages nor of their cunning, and he became the toy of the Navajo negotiators, who distracted him with fine promises of peace and prolonged the agreement as to the location of the peace conference until they had achieved their aims with no trouble and with greatest damage to our citizens, who by taking up arms had abandoned all their interests and even worse, had wasted their time. Señor Pérez thus gave his enemies an opportunity to discredit him by circulating and exaggerating his faults among the people, without considering the consequences.

When in obedience to repeated superior orders Señor Pérez tried to take the first steps toward establishing a direct tax in this department (which these inhabitants had always resisted, based on terms conceded to the settlers who were always subject to the many fatigues, costs, and dangers that they gratuitously suffered) all the permanent troop at that time was sent home for lack of resources, at the same time the caravan from the United States arrived. Perhaps because the proceeds of the caravan were small or because of bad investment or perhaps both together, the result was that the solemn obligations of government were not satisfied, the troops continued in disuse, and the conduct of the favorites of Señor Pérez became each day more unpopular for their indiscretions, their irresponsibility towards their contracts, and their scorn of public opinion and the complaints of the aggrieved. All those concerned in these actions were now disgusted, from those who were truly victims of the administration, to those who had public spirit and those who considered themselves overlooked in promotions in their jobs, and people in general who saw that New Mexico's fortunes were far from being improved and in fact that New Mexico was rushing toward total ruin. The enemies of Señor Pérez made diligent use of these circumstances to alarm the people with exaggerations of the unjust and exhorbitant taxes that were being imposed upon them, persuading them that some were being used for the excesses and illegalities of his favorites, that such taxes were being ordered only by the government at Santa Fe to finance the extravagant behavior of the same employees. As soon as the people were brought to a certain level of discontent, distrust, and exaltation by this means, the tenacious enemies of Señor Pérez planned a revolution that had for its ostensible object only the jobs of the present favorites of Señor Pérez. Intending at first no more than to ask Señor Pérez for these, they joined the more excited people at various points in Río Arriba. Señor Pérez knew perfectly well the authors of these movements and the object they had in mind, which was to destroy him and all his employees, but underestimating the movers and their means, he persisted in following the counsel of his favorites in spite of the opinions of circumspect and well-intentioned people who only longed for the tranquility of the country; he did not arrest the leaders of the revolution nor put the troop under arms, and with only some two hundred men he sallied forth at the head of persons who were in league with his adversaries, believing that with these he could command respect of the rebellious multitude. He marched to battle on the 7th of August, 1837, and the final result was that [crossed-out]: ~~on the 12th of the same Señor Cura Martínez sung the Te Deum Laudamus for him in the Santuario of the Lord of Esquipulas of Chimayó~~ [five words blacked out] the same Señor Pérez, his secretary, the district judge, the perfect of the first district, and various other civil and military officers and other citizens attached to his service were assassinated by their cruel enemies independently of those who fell in battle.

So it was that with best intentions and qualifications and more than ordinary talent and valor a governor and military commander who came from the interior with lack of knowledge of the character of these inhabitants, of their needs, opinions, and traditional concerns, caused a bloody revolution in which he died, and in which even the integrity of the Republic was endangered. These facts I think may be useful not only for telling the future government what happened but also that the facts may not be distorted by what the real authors of the revolution have made available to, among others, Don C. M. B. [probably Carlos María Bustamante, a leading historian of Mexico at that time] for his accounts of the history of Mexico.

Don Manuel Armijo, present governor and commanding general of this department who took command of the lovers of order and of the constitutional government, had the honor of putting down the revolutionary hydra in 1837 and of reestablishing order and peace among us. Here it is proper to compare his administration with that of Señor Pérez who preceded him, and with Don Mariano Martínez who followed him; for with no more than the same resources of those two other men, he had the good fortune of maintaining peace in New Mexico and making it respected in the exterior more than at any other time since Independence, but since this gentleman rules the destiny of the country at present, it would appear flattery on my part to relate his services, so I will limit myself to saying that he controlled the revolutionaries with moral or physical force on two occasions, and captured the invading Texans, and made New Mexico respected by the Indians that surround it, much more than in the two epochs I referred to, and perhaps more than in any other since Independence. . . .

(Mexican Archives of New Mexico [MANM], microfilm roll 21, frames 340–45).

3.   An Account of the Chimayó Rebellion, 1837

The following manuscript account was written for an unidentified newspaper at an unknown date, and signed only "one who loves his country." Evidence points to Albino Chacón as its author. The author describes himself as "a former member of the government, now retired"; Chacón was second alcalde of Santa Fe during Governor Pérez's administration and retired after Pérez's death, in August 1837, but was again alcalde of Santa Fe by October 21. The account was probably written between September 21, when the Taos faction surrendered to Manuel Armijo and the author assumed that the rebellion was over, and October 18, when the Truchas uprising showed that the rebellion was still alive. The account was written for a newspaper, but there was no newspaper in New Mexico at this time. It may have been submitted to the government newspaper, *Diario del Gobierno,* and rejected for publication, perhaps because of the author's sarcastic disapproval of the government's neglect of New Mexico.

Albino Chacón was born in 1808, served on the Santa Fe ayuntamiento in the 1830s, became second alcalde of Santa Fe in 1837, and retained that position off and on until 1846. After the American invasion, in August 1846, Chacón moved to Peñasco, near Taos, where he died in 1876. His son Rafael wrote a manuscript autobiography entitled "Memoirs of Major Rafael Chacón," in which he quotes from an "unofficial report" written by his father Albino Chacón to the Minister of War and Navy describing the death of Pérez. The "unofficial report" (part of which is quoted in this paper) is similar to but not the same as "An Account of the Chimayó Rebellion, 1837."

By the turn of the century, both "An Account of the Chimayó Rebellion, 1837" and "Memoirs of Major Rafael Chacón" were in the possession of Rafael's son Eusebio Chacón, of Trinidad, Colorado, from whom Benjamin M. Read obtained copies for use in his *Illustrated History of New Mexico* (1912). The handwritten copy of the manuscript, from which I made the following translation, is deposited in the Benjamin M. Read Collection, State Records Center and Archives, Santa Fe. I have added accents, punctuation and paragraphs where the document needed them.

The supreme government and the public being badly informed by the newspapers of the causes of the revolution in this department, I took the liberty of sending you the following account of what the general opinion and known facts show as most notable about its beginning and the course that it took. As I am independent of the factions that figured in it and permanently resigned from all public office, the only motive that induced me to write it with all impartiality is the desire of making known the true causes of the evils, so that proper remedies may be applied to them. If my weak effort gains your approval and through your newspaper succeeds in contributing something to the end that I have indicated, I will consider myself more than repaid for the little amount of work that it has cost me. And so I say that:

New Mexico, abandoned since the beginning of independence, appeared to have no other relation to the rest of the Republic than a common origin, language, and customs. Its only resource after that was the product of the customs duties that a small annual caravan of North Americans paid on the goods they introduced, which even in the years that yielded best, was never amply sufficient to supply the entire needs of the presidial company from its allotment, nor from that time on was it ever complete. The geographical situation of New Mexico, separated by great distance from the rest of the Republic, surrounded by wild tribes, some of them powerful and warlike, and almost all savage enemies of the inhabitants, was subject to furious attacks of Indian neighbors which love of country and national honor always made the inhabitants resist with firmness, and many times they succeeded in driving them back to the center of their own lands, severely punished. This was always at the cost and fatigue of these same inhabitants, without any help from the general government and not even once with arms and ammunition. During a series of many years of fatigue and sacrifice, the supreme government was informed many times of the critical situation of the country that each day became more alarming, both because the number of enemies was increasing and because they were becoming improved in the art of war; and that they were much better supplied with arms and munitions than the inhabitants of New Mexico, but the supreme government did not come forward because it never paid them any attention; these poor inhabitants with their farms and other resources ruined, lost the enthusiasm and means for making war, and their enemies were encouraged in the same proportion, continuing to commit depredations with impunity on the very outskirts of the settlements. Reduced, then, in spite of such hardship, to the extreme misery in various places of fearing to sow their fields because of the great danger they risked, the people began showing some discontent, as is certainly natural in such unhappiness, during the governorship of Don Francisco Sarracino, not against the system of government nor against the supreme powers of the nation, but against the administration of this gentleman, to whom they attributed all their misfortunes. [1] The poverty of this period was such that the few foot soldiers in service were discharged, and various respectable citizens who were convinced that the ruin of the territory was inevitable, petitioned the governor for passports to move with their families to California. This is the state New Mexico was in when it was known that Colonel Don Albino Pérez was coming as governor, for whom the supreme government had provided distinguished character recommendations. The announcement gave hope of better conditions, as much for the nature of his talent and experience as for the influence of his high rank and connections in the capital of the republic that would obtain from the supreme government the help that New Mexico needed so desperately. The arrival of Pérez at Santa Fe strengthened the image of him that was formed at his announcement. His personal presence, the accounts that his retinue and the gentlemen that had access to him told of the great services he had rendered the country, the actions of war in which he had been distinguished, the plans he had formed to restore the troop of the territory by procuring the wherewithal to maintain it, and to annihilate the Navajos who at that time were attacking constantly, all this generally led to a fine impression of him. In fact, he put the troop under arms and in the beginning made it perform more exact and effective service than ever before; he made the administration more energetic, and in some instances of disputes he gave proof of impartial integrity. When the profits of the caravan were exhausted, he procured help to maintain the troop and employees from the foreign traders under his personal bond, as far as the lenders could extend themselves, but as he could not get enough to continue to support the troop in this way, and getting nothing from Mexico in spite of repeated requests, he turned to the natives of the country who he thought would be able to advance him what he needed by themselves through their own credit. For this reason he was presently seen visiting very frequently the houses of some gentlemen who, without acceding to his solicitation, were convinced of the influence they had and wished to use it in protecting the aims of their ambition. This led to lawsuits and grudges among themselves, and the governor was caught up in their puerile intrigues in spite of himself. Whatever his opinion was in these matters, he could not control all the selfish interests, from which sprung enmities and designs damaging in themselves and to the governor, distracting his attention with the schemes and gossip that occupied them constantly. Lacking means to sustain the soldiers under arms, he had to discharge them to find their subsistence as best they could, and the employees and officers were reduced to what their individual credit or the governor could procure for them, in case there was not sufficient to maintain their ranks. This, along with the ill will of some individuals, gave place to recriminations, each imputing the general calamity to the other. Some employees were accused of infidelity and corruption in their conduct. There were suspensions of employees and also parties gotten up to support or ruin distinguished persons; and finally everything was a mess.[2]

The Navajo tribe at the same time was not idle, committing depredations of every kind in every place, capturing persons and driving off great numbers of stock, burning various persons alive in their houses, and committing murders around Santa Fe, the best-guarded jurisdiction in the territory. All with impunity. It is true that among other campaigns the governor led a general one against the Navajos in person, but it produced no more effect than to lose most of the animals they had, and thus ruin many unfortunate farmers. In the midst of so many misfortunes, the people sought the cause of their misery; some attributed it to the corruption and bad management of the employees, circulating accusations that the complainants were spreading; others blamed the governor who with the number of officers that accompanied him, consumed the property of the troop that, well-directed, could have defended the territory. The most impartial persons considered in fact that the administration and coming of Señor Pérez to New Mexico had actually increased all the evils, both by the rapid consumption of the scarce resources of the country in the salaries of his retinue, and in the quarreling and intrigue that he tolerated in his administration, without producing any good whatever that his qualifications and good intentions had promised. The new constitution arrived when the people were already so oppressed with misery and had such a bad opinion of the administration, that when they saw with disgust that they had to pay taxes, which they supposed were used only in sustaining the luxury and waste of a few individuals of Santa Fe, they did not stop to consider advantages and disadvantages that the constitution itself might have.

When in obedience to the constitution elections and appointments were carried out as ordered, a spirit of inordinate ambition was noted with some intrigues and combinations that had not been seen here before (except when used by Señor Barreiro to get elected deputy) and the result therefore left many doleful aspirants who expressed rather publicly the injustice they claimed to have received in disregard of their seniority.[3] The appointment of Don Ramón Abréu as prefect of the first district was perhaps the most fitting, for he was a citizen who since youth had been employed in the public business in which he had acquired much instruction and experience, and was perhaps the most competent to discharge with propriety this most important position. He was also the one most displeasing to many gentlemen who believed they should have been preferred for their wealth, respectability, and prestige. Various of these gentlemen who lost no occasion to criticize his appointment, pursued their determination to such a point that they succeeded in making Don Ramón Abréu unpopular in the jurisdiction where he lived and they proposed to separate him from the position by every means possible so that he would resign out of weariness. With this object they spread among the people and particularly the common people the most atrocious calumnies against the governor and prefect concerning plans they had made to rob the people of as much as they possessed with appearance of legality, saying that the arbitrary and unregulated collection of taxes in Santa Fe was no more than a petty demonstration of what these officials intended to do;[4] that the constitution and division of the republic into departments was not the doing of the sovereign congress but of the magnates in Santa Fe and of the prefect; and they gave the constitution the most absurd and malign interpretation that a rational being could imagine. Informed of the public opinion in general and particularly with respect to taxes, or rather believing that the Supreme Government would exempt New Mexico from being a department and from paying taxes because of the peculiarity of its situation and its poverty, the governor took no steps to collect taxes nor even to consider the matter, fearing no doubt that it would cause some popular commotion (little did he know how much!) and he awaited supreme resolution.[5] By this time the caravan of North Americans were here and preparing to return to their country, for which reason the creditors of the public treasury had to collect what was owed to them from the government grain supply, under contracts now due. The employees put them off saying that they had not yet adjusted the accounts, and that the terms that the laws conceded to the traders had not expired, but the creditors knew that most of them had already paid all their customs duties and they saw that all the profit was wasted in extravagant luxury and gambling. Tired of their long residence in Santa Fe, they repeated their demands with more force, stating what they knew about the matter, and that some three thousand pesos had been paid to Don J. E. Pino, whom they feared had less right to it than they themselves. The supreme head of the treasury, Don Francisco Sarracino, not having anything to say to them nor perhaps anything to pay them with, avoided their complaints by posting in the corners of the plaza a notice prohibiting the creditors from appearing in the office of the treasury for 20 days so that the adjustment of their manifests, which was being done in preference to all other business, might not be interrupted by their importunities. After this announcement, which appeared to everyone to add insult to injury, it happened that on the same night various Treasury employees gambled away sums of money that neither their salaries nor their fortunes justified; moreover they knew very well what was the product of the importation duties. Seeing this with resentment and desperation in their breasts, the traders left Santa Fe for home the following day, telling their acquaintances on the journey what had happened to them and what they had witnessed. As most of the creditors were from Taos these actual circumstances gave validity to the calumnies that were circulating now in the jurisdiction of Río Arriba, and contributed a great deal to alienate many persons of influence from the governor. Perhaps in [New] Mexico tranquility would have prevailed in spite of such discontents and traumas that have just been referred to, except for an incident that happened in the Villa of Santa Cruz de la Cañada, that most excitable and rebellious settlement in all the territory. What happened was this:

Among those from New Mexico who were in the interior of the republic to sell their work of wool and leather, was a Taos man named Víctor Sánchez, along with some men from La Cañada who had been detained for having failed to bring customs house permits, not knowing they were required. These men, to avoid loss, asked and received permission of Sánchez to deliver their goods to him so that he might make the necessary arrangements and finish the business as best he could. Sánchez had to pay out some money and the *asesor* [legal advisor] of Chihuahua gave him a testimonial in due form so that he could collect from his companions what they owed him. Sánchez went to receive payment from them, and all of them denied having done it. He brought action against them before the alcalde of La Cañada, Esquibel, and this man refused to administer justice on frivolous pretexts. Sánchez then appeared before the governor, and this gentleman decreed that Sánchez present himself before the prefect of the first district who was the proper authority to hear the business; Sánchez did so, and the prefect ordered that the alcalde of La Cañada administer the justice that he sought, according to the document that he presented. As the defendants were of the faction that had made Esquibel alcalde and his election had been a pure riot, Esquibel did not think it advisable to work against the defendants and he disobeyed the prefect. After various altercations in which

Esquibel used disrespectful language, he refused to obey the prefect and challenged him to punish him if he could, being an alcalde placed by the wish of the jurisdiction to administer justice as he understood it, and the prefect being an authority unrecognized by the people and without right to command them. When the matter came to this extreme the prefect successively suspended Esquibel, arrested him, fined him, ordered him placed in irons, and increased the fine to 30 pesos. The knave Esquibel who without doubt purposely provoked these punishments, instigated by some villains and by his own perversity, by knowing the spirit of that jurisdiction, stirred up by individuals who did not care what means they used to achieve their sinister purposes, counting on the faction that had made him alcalde, he was set free at the end of July by some other factions. Declaring himself openly an enemy of established order and of the authorities, he formed a council called "Cantón" with twelve villains from among the hotheads as its voting members, and with the secret help of other citizens who directed it. He confirmed all the calumnies and fantasies as they had circulated to the public; he invented laws, orders, plans, and letters from the authorities that he pretended he had intercepted on the subject of the same imputations already cited, which he had published in various places and sent them to all the jurisdictions where he counted on supporters. In one of his first sessions, counting now on the excitement, he decided among other things to demand that Señor Pérez sign a paper to deliver up to the rebels his secretary, the judge of the district, and the prefect of the First District to be shot, which is sufficient indication that they were influenced by those who could take advantage of the vacancies. The Cantón made a very absurd kind of declaration of its principles and aims, identifying itself with the name of *the faith of Jesus Christ*. By these means, under the mask of religion, they perpetrated outrages, seduced the common people of Río Arriba, the Indians of various pueblos, and even people who were considered honorable. They used so much diligence and activity that within a few days they had an important force which they made use of to compel those perons to join who would voluntarily not wish to contribute to the upheavals and disorders that they foresaw; these they now stigmatized as traitors. The governor believed at the beginning (in spite of many warnings) that the disturbances of La Cañada were nothing to worry about, and he knew that he could placate them with no more than reproaches and threats, while he wasted precious time that the Cantón knew how to use for getting prepared, engaging the multitude, and sowing discord in the rest of the territory. So when the governor tried to collect a force sufficient to subdue the rebels he encountered very few people who wanted to accompany him, protesting that business and illness prevented them. The alcaldes, perhaps on purpose or because the people refused to serve, did not present more than a small party of the men who were sought from them, and finally with the greatest exertion some two hundred men were gathered, most of them Indians. With this weak force, trusting no doubt that they would not have to fight, the governor left Santa Fe on August 7. On the following day the two forces sighted each other at a distance near La Mesilla of San Ildefonso, and when the governor ordered the people to get into formation and was preparing to enter into discussion with the rebels, who were divided into four factions, men of the third faction posted on a ridge to the left fired their guns which was supposedly a signal for the rebels to attack. They attacked, in fact, at the same instant that a large party of the governor's people and all the Indians with their alcaldes passed over to the other side.

Most of the rebel force charged on a few faithful men defending a cannon ["three cannon" crossed out] who, although they did their duty, succumbed to the mob which took them prisoner, having first killed 7 men and wounded many others. The governor with 23 individuals who remained loyal made an honorable retreat to Santa Fe, where it was said publicly and aloud that they had been abandoned and the good cause lost. The fourth party of rebels (whose identifying principle is unknown) were the authors of the revolution and of the evils that necessarily must afflict New Mexico. In the same night the governor left from Santa Fe with some gentlemen and employees that the Cantón had already marked as victims. On the 9th the Cantón arrived at the little capital of Santa Fe, and on the same and the following day the governor and most of those who left with him on the night of the 8th were killed. The governor traveled toward Río Abajo until he met a force of militia in charge of the rebel Don A. Antonito Chávez who refused him any protection, which is why, as he was returning to Santa Fe, he was killed by two Indians in its suburbs, and his head carried to the camp and jeered by the perverted villains. Don Ramón Abréu, Don M.no [Marcelino] Abreu, Don J. M. Alaríd and others were taken prisoner and conducted by the Indians to the camp, but the barbarous and bloody Cantón feared so much that some circumstance would preserve their lives that it ordered immediately that all of them be instantly killed. Don S. Abréu and Alférez Saenz were killed the following day at Santo Domingo. So great was the indolence and incompetence of the authorities of Santa Fe that by order of a detachment of the Cantón they sought out Lieutenant Colonel Don Manuel Aponte who was hidden in a house badly wounded, and was surrendered up with the understanding that he would be killed. The people and more particularly the soldiers hated to witness this surrender, already ashamed of the situation in which they had been placed. They could scarcely hide their indignation, knowing that they could do nothing to avoid the surrender nor save the honor of the city. On the 10th, after holding the election of governor which devolved on a farmer named José Gonzales whose only talent was knowing how to kill buffalo, they entered Santa Fe. The first act of the new governor this day was to distribute among the worthy of the faction as much as was then known to belong to those who had just been assassinated, and two people who did not care to be taken for members of this party received jewelry as creditors of the dead governor, although it was public and notorious that neither one nor the other had any account or business with said gentleman. One of these same two who had been distinguished already in outrages against the head of Señor Pérez in the camp, had the brutal insolence to put on the dolman that had been worn by Señor Pérez when he was killed, making himself conspicuous by pointing out the hole of the ball that had killed him, and whistling to those that he believed were his friends. After this day Santa Fe and the rest of New Mexico was in a state of confusion and terror with no more law in force than the wishes of the friends of the governor and of the Cantón, for in spite of having established what they called a government, the Cantón did not wish to be dissolved but continued to take revolutionary measures at times contrary to those of Gonzales, persecuting and threatening with death those who had been opposed to the rebellion and those they thought had not approved of their aims. They had the jail of La Cañada full of innocent folk and still they summoned to their tribunal numberless individuals on whom they wished to satiate their fury. On the 27th of August, Gonzales, or rather his faction, made a formal division of all the property that he could recover from the dead, to the injury of their families and numerous creditors, among them many people charged with reestablishing order and the laws. Gonzales departed, which in fact lifted the public spirit rather swiftly, so that on the 7th of September the soldiers with the same feelings as the citizens, demanded their arms and offered to serve without pay, in order to prevent, as they said, another insult similar to that which the Cantón inflicted on them in the person of Lieutenant Colonel Aponte, and after that day they did service and military drill morning and afternoon. A few days later news arrived at Santa Fe of the pronouncement of Tomé, which was due to the virtues, patriotism, and talents actively displayed by the gentlemen who signed it.

This communication which included the election of Don Man.l Armijo as chief of the armed force, was received in Santa Fe with heartfelt cheering and acclamations that showed the territory that its citizens and troops were firmly decided in favor of the good cause. On the 10th Gonzales returned from Taos as if fleeing from that Cantón, and scarcely had he dismounted from his horse than he was notified by the civil and military authorities of the determination they had made and their adhesion to the pronouncement of Tomé, and that he must surrender because of suspension of the government that the rebels had set up. A few days later Don Manuel Armijo arrived with the armed citizens of Río Abajo, the most respectable men, as was noted, of that jurisdiction. The conduct that officers and soldiers observed while remaining in Santa Fe was worthy of all praise. There was no example of a lack of discipline and all the citizenry remained very pleased at the deportment of their guests, and showed consideration to the number of 800 men; it is the major proof of the morality and good spirit that animated them. The Cantón of Taos gathered a multitude of more than 3,000 men of all classes, but as it always happens when defending a bad cause, they were without unity, without regulation, and without direction. Señor Armijo was informed of the state of that force which although numerous was weak because of the element that composed it, and certain of conquering it, he used policy to avoid the effusion of blood among brothers of the same country. So wise were his measures that he succeeded without shedding a drop of blood; the Cantón itself delivered the principal ringleaders recognized from the first revolution through a treaty signed in Santa Fe on the 21st of September, 1837, and disarmed by this act the hydra of the revolution that threatened to devastate New Mexico.

The dereliction of the Supreme Government, the distractions, corruption, and ineptitude of the authorities of Santa Fe and the spirit of inordinate ambition recognized for a long time in some individuals, had contributed to the reproduction of the spirit in the breasts of the most docile, industrious and good inhabitants in the entire republic. The measures that the Supreme Government took in an event so transcendental indicated its wisdom and the great importance it ascribes to this territory, because perhaps, full of benevolence, it might have been satisfied with seeing it disarmed and impotent, or perhaps, full of severity, it might have punished the perpetrators with vigor, but it takes a very different course with respect to this country, which even here will rise again from its ashes. There will always be too many unhappy people who, not having protection or justice from the authorities, may risk their lives at the call of whatever ambitious fellow offers himself to them, hoping to better their lot and not afraid of losing, whatever the results may be, so I think one can deduce from this account that it is not the force of principle that spread discontent but the disorders of the governed and the misery of the public, ignored by those who have the obligation to remedy it. This is the opinion and fear of

One who loves his country.

1. Sarracino was officially governor from April 18, 1833, to May 22, 1835.

2. Benjamin M. Read in his *Illustrated History of New Mexico*, p. 372, translates part of this last sentence, which reads in Spanish: "partes para sostener y para perder señalados personas" as "parties were designated to assassinate certain designated persons," giving an erroneous meaning to the phrase, I believe.

3. Antonio Barreiro was the asesor, or legal advisor, to the government of New Mexico from 1831 to 1835, when he was elected deputy from New Mexico to the General Congress (Treasurer of Mexico to the Treasurer of New Mexico, July 21, 1838, MANM roll 25, 901–2). Among other means of winning his election, he started the first short-lived New Mexican newspaper, *El Crepúsculo de la Libertad.*

4. The author here refers to a municipal ordinance passed by the Santa Fe ayuntamiento on June 9, 1836, taxing wagons, animals, and stores of foreign merchants, as well as entertainments such as dances, performances, etc. (Read, *Illustrated History*, pp. 373–74n). Read confuses this city tax with the federal taxes demanded under the departmental plan and cites it as a principal cause of rebellion.

5. The governor discussed the matter with his subcomisario. see "The Departmental Plan," above.

4. Letter of Manuel Armijo, September 12, 1837

After Armijo had collected his men and arms and was ready to march on the rebels at Santa Fe, he wrote this letter from his camp at Bernalillo to his commanding officer at Chihuahua and to the minister of war at Mexico City. The letter was published in the government newspaper on October 19. The first three or four paragraphs were written by the editor, as can be seen by references to "documents that the Supreme Government has received," "that department," and "assassins of the North." Somewhere in the middle of the fourth paragraph, the words of Manuel Armijo take over to describe the disaster, and they are brisk, simple, and self-effacing, unlike the bombast for which he was noted.

MEXICO, 12 September 1837. With the most profound sorrow we insert today the documents that the Supreme Government has received relating to the barbarous and execrable revolution that has stained New Mexico with blood. The most excellent governor Don Alvino Pérez, other functionaries of that department, and various citizens faithful to their duty have been victims of some monsters who appear to have taken as a model of conduct the impiety and fierceness of the savage tribes who inhabit the larger part of that territory.

Beyond the veil of confusion and darkness that still covers the motives and circumstances of this unspeakable crime, it is already perceived as one which inflames with holy indignation the breast of every Mexican and of every man possessed of the most ordinary feelings of humanity and patriotism. Assassination the means and infamous treason the object of their rebellion, such are the titles that the political reformers of New Mexico claim for the abomination of a humane and generous people who are ashamed that such cannibals have sullied the name of Mexicans, which they do not deserve.

Horrible, execrable have been these acts of atrocity, the only recognizable motive being the satisfaction of personal hatred exasperated by violence and injustice. But the assassins of the North lack even this dismal excuse: after ferociously immolating their lawful authorities and many of their fellow citizens, they have put the seal on their iniquity with the greatest of crimes, and renouncing the sacred chains which united them to their country by laws, blood, and religion, they attempt to rend the national colors by substituting the shameful symbol of foreign domination.

We would insult the nation if we were to doubt that such crimes will raise in all parts of the Republic a universal cry of censure and anger. The Supreme Government is very actively occupied in dictating measures for the pacification of New Mexico, and will inexorably cause the sword of the law to fall on assassins and traitors. The horror of their crimes would have disgraced the best of causes. Will they find pardon and friendly feeling because their cause is the greatest of crimes? One that used the ignorance of the common people to make them believe that the departmental laws were against all natural and divine right, that they must divide with the government half of all they possess, even to their children, with a thousand other absurdities too many to recount, but which made such an impression on their minds that they were alarmed immediately and are still suffering from the evils that provoked such a rebellion. The result was that the governor could not placate them with lenience; he had a very small force composed mostly of Indians from the Cochití, Santo Domingo, and Sandía pueblos who instead of being of benefit, were a detriment to him. They deserted to the other side and then attacked him with the rest of the rebels, leaving him no more than thirty men with whom he had to make an honorable retreat to the capital with the loss of seventeen dead and a number of wounded, among them Brevet Lieutenant Colonel Don José Manuel Aponte, who for his heroism "in the words of the officers who escaped" is worthy of the president's consideration.

Not content with their triumph, nor wishing to hear the

voice of reason and justice, the rebels unloosed all their fury against the governor, and on the ninth of August they followed him on the road he had taken out of Santa Fe to Santo Domingo, and, deaf and disobedient to his orders, they killed him, although with considerable difficulty because of the vigorous defense he made, and they did the same with impunity to his aide, Lieutenant Hurtado, to the prefect of the first district, to the judge of the treasury Don Santiago Abréu, to the secretary of government, and to three others of his company.

Until now I have shown your excellency a disaster caused by disobedience, but the results of it, arising from the ignorant becoming experienced, are the most terrible, and are those that have made the sensible men I have the honor to command take up arms; having taken no part in the rebellion, they are trying to reduce to order innumerable unhappy people who remain deceived, and to punish their ringleaders according to law, the result of which will be communicated to you as soon as it is achieved. For the present I will only tell you that the Department of New Mexico has not been disloyal but only suppressed by a rioting mob from which it could not free itself because of the bloody measures the mob employed, and for this reason I believe there has been no opportunity to tell you what I have just related.

The Mexican government must be persuaded that if New Mexico has had men of contemptible nature capable of committing horrible assassinations of the governor and his employees, it also has honorable and faithful men determined to wash away this ominous stain with their blood and make the laws the sole guide of their operations; according to these same laws, the pronouncement of the 8th of the current month was made without hesitation, as will be seen in the accompanying act. I only hope that your excellence approves, and that prompt help may be sought from the commanding general of Chihuahua who, as my immediate superior, has also received knowledge of all that occurred.

I have the honor to offer myself to you with all respect and submission.

God and law. General Quarters, Bernalillo, September 12, 1837.—Manuel Armijo.

Most excellent Minister of War and Navy. Copied, Mexico, October 13, 1837. *Mora.*

(*Diario del Gobierno de la República Méxicana,* vol. 9, no. 903, Oct. 19, 1837, p. 48.)

5. Testimony of Merchants, August 28, 1837

At dawn on August 28, 1837, a caravan of merchants arrived at El Paso del Norte from Santa Fe with news so electrifying that the commander of El Paso del Norte took the testimony of three of the merchants and sent it immediately by *extraordinario violento* to the district commander at Chihuahua, who forwarded it to Mexico City. The testimony was published in the *Diario del Gobierno* and provides us with another view of the rebellion. Juan García was a merchant of El Paso del Norte, with a name so common as to defy further identification. Guadalupe Miranda was an important man in Republican New Mexico. Although Miranda states that in 1837 he was a farmer of El Paso del Norte, he had lived in New Mexico in 1829 and taught school in Santa Fe in 1832 and perhaps later. In 1841 he and Charles Beaubien were given a land grant by Manuel Armijo, which was later famous as the Maxwell Grant. At this time he was serving as Armijo's secretary, although by 1844 he was back in El Paso del Norte, where he served as alcalde in 1845. He remained there as a citizen of Mexico after the United States invasion, and was commissioner of emigration for Mexico in 1853, attempting to induce New Mexicans to emigrate to Mexico.

Josiah Gregg first came as a Santa Fe trader to New Mexico in 1831 and visited it nearly every summer afterwards until 1839. His famous book, *Commerce of the Prairies*, has found frequent reference herein.

The use of the word *pueblo* is well illustrated in the testimony. It has four meanings—people in general; town; an adobe village of the Pueblo Indians; a Pueblo Indian. These definitions are interchangeable in some contexts. When Manuel Armijo addressed a speech in 1846 to "Pueblos!" he could have meant people, towns, and Pueblo Indians all at once. But when Guadalupe Miranda speaks in his testimony of "el pueblo de la villa Sta. Cruz de Cañada reunido y resuelto a oponerse a las ordenes dictadas por suprefectura," he is speaking of the people—for a town does not meet and resolve to oppose the subprefecture's orders. However, a few sentences later when Miranda writes of the "fuerzas de los pueblos del río abajo," he is referring to the Pueblo Indians of Río Abajo, who were the only people recruited from Río Abajo for Pérez's forces. Later Miranda writes about the "indigenas y vecinos de los pueblos de Cochití y Santa Domingo"—the natives (Indians) and Hispanic residents of Cochití and Santo Domingo pueblos, plainly referring in this case to the adobe complexes and not the people. The confusion over the ethnic origin of Governor José Gonzales is probably a result of the many meanings of this ubiquitous word.

Testimony of Juan García, Guadalupe Miranda, and Josias Gregg, August 28, 1837. Official despatch. General Government. Minister of War and Navy. General command of the internal department of the north.—Most excellent sir. —Lieutenant Colonel Don Cayetano Justiniani on the 28th of August last by extraordinario violento says to me the following:

"Commanding General.—the declarations attached will inform you of the revolution and disasters originating in the Department of New Mexico. They are of such magnitude that they oblige me to give you knowledge of them by extraordinario violento, so that you may be informed and pleased to pass the news to the most excellent governor, that you and he may immediately dictate suitable measures to save and secure that district from a coming invasion that the authors of this one will naturally launch against it, satisfied that it has no force for its defence; you may be sure that if the factions try such a thing before I receive the aid I expect, I will be sacrificed for my country before succumbing to their wretched ideas, which in my opinion are the same as those of the perverse adventurers of Texas.

"—I am left with my means of defence which, although weak, will be sufficient if the need arises to maintain the Mexican reputation."

I am sending this letter to your excellency along with copies of the declarations cited, so that you may give an account of this unhappy event to the most excellent president, showing him that in order to contain such evils, aid of every kind will be required, assuring his excellency that in the meantime while waiting to receive it, I will stay on the defensive and prepare to take the offensive with the few resources that I can rely on, making, therefore, every effort to maintain the integrity of the department and the honor of the Mexican flag whatever happens. God and Liberty. Chihuahua, September 12, 1837.—At ten in the night.—José J. Calvo. —Most excellent Minister of War and Navy

Military command of the district.—At this moment, which is seven in the morning, I have been advised that citizens of this village Juan García and Guadalupe Miranda have arrived from New Mexico, communicating that all the people of that department have revolted, killing their principal authorities and other respectable individuals, committing forthwith all the crimes and excesses of which a disordered people is capable. You will immediately take the declarations of these said individuals, investigating through them the origin of such disasters, giving immediate account of the results to the commanding general of this department. God and Liberty. Villa del Paso 28 August 1837.—*Cayetano Justiniani.*—*Don Tomás Zuloaga.*

The citizen Tomás Zuloaga, captain of the permanent company of San Elceario and judge appointed for the following proceedings.—Having named a scribe according to the general ordinances of the army so that I may actuate said proceedings that I am going to execute according to the above order of the prefect and military commander of this district, Lieutenant Colonel Don Cayetano Justiniani, I name Juan Padilla, corporal of the same company, to exercise the position of scribe, and having advised him of the obligation he contracts, he accepts, swears and protests that he will maintain secrecy and fidelity in all he does, and so that it may be of record, he signed with me in the Villa del Paso on the 28th of August, 1837.—*Tomás Zuloaga.*—*Juan Padilla.*

At once the same public prosecutor made to appear before him Don Juan García, resident of this villa who has just arrived from the department of New Mexico, whom I, the present scribe, made to raise his right hand and asked him, do you swear before God and the sovereignty of the nation to tell the truth about what I shall ask you? He so swears. Asked his name, employment, and when he arrived at this villa? He says: that his name is as given above; that he is resident and farmer of this same villa, and that he arrived at dawn of this day. Asked if he knows what occurrences have taken place in the department of New Mexico in regard to a conspiracy that those people executed against their authorities, what the origin of these disorders was, with what aims they were directed, what persons have died at the hands of the factions, and that he tell in detail as much as he knows about it: He says: that being in the capital of the department of New Mexico for mercantile purposes on the third of this month, he knew through some residents and also through public rumor that the people of Río Arriba including the Villa of Santa Cruz de Cañada had been aroused against the first authority, in consequence of not wishing to obey the orders of the prefect of their district: the following day he saw that a party of 98 men of the pueblos of Río Abajo arrived at that capital to help the most excellent governor Don Alvino Pérez who was already preparing to march to Santa Cruz de la Cañada with the object of bringing those people to order, for which purpose he was just then publishing a proclamation in which he warned the inhabitants of this city that at the ringing of bells or firing of cannon they should gather with their arms in the principal plaza to enlist; that at eight at night of the same day the declarant undertook his march, leaving that town in complete disorder and alarm, and finally, he could state with certainty that, according to what he observed as he passed among the people, all were in agreement with the rebels: that he does not know any other origin for these disorders nor the aims to which they were directed: that it is evident from a letter sent to Don Guadalupe Miranda (who came in the convoy with the declarant) that the revolution has been realized and that it is certain that the following people have perished: The governor Colonel Don Alvino Pérez, Don Santiago Abréu, district judge, Don Ramón Abréu, prefect of the district of the capital, Don Jesús María Alarid, secretary of government, Francisco Sarracino, treasurer, Lieutenant of infantry Don José Hurtado, Alférez Don Diego Sáenz, Don Antonio Sena, Don Marcelino Abréu, Don Miguel Sena, Don Juan Bustamante, Don Juan López, and various others; wounded was Lieutenant Colonel Don Manuel Aponte: that is all he knows about it, that he has no more to add and that it is the truth in keeping with the oath he made in which the declaration was affirmed and ratified as read to him; and says he is 29 years old and signs it with the present scribe.—*Tomás de Zuloaga.*—*Juan García.*—*Before me, Juan Padilla.*

Immediately on the said day, month, and year, the said public prosecutor made to appear before him Don Guadalupe Miranda, resident of this villa who has just arrived from the department of New Mexico, to whom before me the present scribe he raises his right hand and is asked: Do you swear to God and promise in the sovereignty of the nation to tell the truth about what you are going to be asked? He said, I so swear. Asked his name, employment, and when he arrived at this villa. He says: that he is named as above, and that he is a farmer and resident of this villa, and that he arrived at dawn today. Asked if he knows what occurrences have taken place in the department of New Mexico in regard to a conspiracy that those people have executed against their authorities: what the origin of these disorders was: if he knows with what aims they were directed: what persons were present or at the head of the rebels: who were killed at the hands of these factions, and that he tell in detail as much as he knows about it. He said: that from the first to the third of the current month when he was in the capital of that department he observed that the people of the Villa of Santa Cruz de la

Cañada were assembled and resolved to oppose at all costs the orders dictated by their prefecture, because of not being in agreement with the appointment of Don Ramón Abréu and with the taxes imposed by general laws which the most excellent governor Don Alvino Pérez required to be carried out, for which this magistrate began to take measures, collecting forces from the towns of Río Abajo. So that with them and the majority of citizens who could gather together, they would march to said villa and bring the rebels to order: that the same day of the third, seeing the disorder of those people, the declarant resolved to leave that capital and march for this villa with the convoy of inhabitants who had left that territory with commercial aims: and that along the way at the Pueblo of Sandía he was overtaken by an extraordinario violento sent by the governor for forces to be sent to his aid, since the circumstances now required such haste, it was done in the shortest possible time, ordering up all possible forces: that having continued his march he was passed by some residents of the same who were going to help those authorities, who said to him that the governor had already left Santa Fe with Indians and vecinos of the towns of Cochití and Santo Domingo on the way to the Villa of Santa Cruz de la Cañada where the dissidents were gathered, and not having been able to convince them with reason, hostilities broke out on both sides and in this act the forces of the government [seven words illegible], for which reason the governor and those who remained loyal saw the necessity of escaping from the clutches of their adversaries, but these, without losing a moment, sent various parties in pursuit, catching up with them on the flat mesa of Santo Domingo and sacrificing the governor Don Alvino Pérez and various of his retinue, taking others of them to the pueblo of Santo Domingo where they were decapitated, leaving others dead

114

where the action had taken place and as he was assured, their deaths were horrible: later a servant passed with a letter for the declarant in which there was some news concerning the event, and he shows it to the present judge so that it may advantageously be added to the proceedings, and also a sealed letter sent to Don Agustín Avellano, resident merchant of Chihuahua, which will provide other interesting news: within three or four days of receiving the letters, the foreigner Don Josias Gregg, an Anglo-American, caught up with the declarant and related to him what he knew, assuring him of the death of Don Alvino Pérez and the rest of the individuals who were: Don Santiago Abréu, district judge shot down in the Pueblo of Santo Domingo with two others; Don Ramón Abréu, prefect of the district of the capital, Don Jesús María Alaríd, secretary of government, Francisco Sarracino, treasurer, Lieutenant Don Manuel Hurtado, Alférez Don Diego Sáenz, Don Antonio Sena, Don Marcelino Abréu, Don Miguel Sena, Don Juan Bustamante, Don Juan López, and various other citizens who died in the action of La Cañada and in the dispersion afterwards in company with the said leader, and that according to another Anglo-American whom Gregg talked to along the way, he encountered on the mesa of Santo Domingo the cadaver of Don Alvino Pérez, shot down and his head cut off: that although the declarant does not know the aims that directed this revolution, it will be seen that the governor elected by the factions, José María Gonzalez, vecino of Taos, is an idiot not worthy or capable of filling the position he has usurped, and even less for having been enthroned over the cadavers of the true and legitimate authorities; various decrees dictated by him have been sanctioned and he has invited various foreigners to enlist and march to the United States of the North along with other natives of the country with the sole object of inviting the cabinet in his name to admit the department of New Mexico to join the stars [and stripes], to which the stranger Alicon Estanley [Elisha Stanley] did not care to accede; in addition to this, the declarant had news from some vecinos who caught up with him in his journey that the Lieutenant Colonel Don José María Ronquillo had gone out to meet the dissidents with a white flag signifying peace and offering them his services, demonstrating to them that he was on their side: and this is as much as he knows about the matter; that he has no more to add, and that his testimony is the truth in keeping with his oath, and the declaration was affirmed and ratified as read to him; and he says he is 27 years old and he signs it with the said gentleman and the present scribe. *Tomás de Zuloaga.—Guadalupe Miranda. —Before me, Juan Padilla.*

Immediately the said prosecuting attorney made to appear before him Don Josias Gregg, mentioned in the declaration that preceded this one, who before me the present scribe received his oath according to the form of law, to say the truth about the point on which I am going to interrogate you. He said: I so swear. Asked his name, employment, and whether he can speak Spanish. He says: that he is named as already mentioned; that he is a merchant and knows Spanish. Asked: if he knows what happened in the department of New Mexico concerning a conspiracy that those people carried out against their authorities, and describe it in detail? He says: that from the 1st to the 5th of the current month they were making some preparations to bring to order the vecinos of the towns of Arriba that had gathered in the villa of Santa Cruz de la Cañada to the number of 1,000 to 1,500 men, in consequence of not being in agreement with governmental orders of the prefect of that district, Don Ramón Abréu about collection of the taxes established by the general laws of the whole Republic, so that the same Abréu assured him in private conversation that the most excellent governor Don Alvino Pérez ordered forces gathered from the pueblos of Abajo, and on the 7th began his march from Santa Fe with about 150 men directed towards the aforesaid villa of La Cañada: that on the following day the declarant left for this villa, and on the way he heard that before arriving at said point of La Cañada Don Alvino Pérez had been attacked by the enemy forces with scarcely any warning, and that at the same time the government troops with a cannon passed over to swell the ranks of the opposite side: that the aforesaid governor, with about 25 men who had remained loyal, was able to escape; but the enemy immediately sent parties in pursuit, catching up with said governor in the suburbs of the capital at Santa Fe where, despite the size of the mob, he defended himself vigorously with only the dagger that remained to him, having already shot off his firearms: but in the end he was overcome by force and perished, immediately losing his head which was thrown in the middle of the principal plaza.. This happened on the 9th; on the 10th Don Santiago Abréu and Alférez Don Diego Sáenz were decapitated or assassinated, having been held prisoners since the day before, and gentlemen also apprehended and sacrified were Don Ramón Abréu, Don Marcelino Abreu, Don Manuel Hurtado, Don J. Soto, and another person whose name he does not remember. He also knows that other vecinos were killed in the action, and that Lieutenant Colonel Aponte and Don Francisco Sarracino were gravely wounded. Asked also if he knows who remained in charge of the government provisionally, and what measures he took? He said, that he knows positively that Lieutenant Colonel Don José María Ronquillo remained in charge of the military and politicial command in the absence of Don Alvino Pérez; and since the declarant had already departed the day of the mob attack, he could not be sure of more than he has already expressed; but he knows that the same Ronquillo had left that city on the road to meet the factions with a white flag, in order to congratulate them and offer them his services: that although he does not know who the movers of the revolution were, in passing the town of Tomé Padre Don Francisco Madariaga told him that on that date José Gonzalez was in command of the government, a resident of the town of Taos ["vecino del pueblo de Taos"], a man without civil virtues and so ignorant that he does not even know how to sign his name; that although it is not apparent who the movers of the conspiracy were, it was certain that men in high places in that department directed the operations of the factions secretly and without showing their faces: that he has nothing more to add and that what he says is the truth, according to the oath taken, in which the declaration was affirmed and ratified as read to him: and he signs it with the said gentlemen and the present scribe.—*Tomás de Zuloaga.* —*Josias Gregg.*

Immediately, on said day, month, and year, the public prosecutor of these proceedings just concluded, went in presence of the scribe to the lodging of the military commander of this district, Leiutenant Colonel Don Cayetano Justiniani, to deliver the present proceedings composed of ten pages used, one blank, and also a letter added to the original file. It was done: and so that it may be recorded, said gentlemen signs it, of which I the undersigned scribe attest.—*Zuloaga.* —*Juan Padilla*

August 12, 1837. Esteemed friend: since as a rule no mail goes out from here I have the presumption to ask you to place the enclosed [illegible word] in the El Paso post office.—It is likely that you already know the disaster that the revolution of Río Arriba has caused: after defeating the governor and the Abréus at La Cañada, they caught up with them on the mesa of Santo Domingo, and killed them: the same happened to Sarracino at La Cañada: it is likely that Aponte died as a result of very grave wounds that he received in the action. Much death, much revolution, and much disorder there is. God help us to enlighten those who have sought to ruin their country.—Please excuse the presumption that as a friend I beg of you, your affectionate friend Q.B.S.M. [who kisses your hand]. Copied from the original proceedings sent by the military commander of El Paso. —*Antonio Rey, secretary.*

(*Diario del Gobierno de la República Mexicana,* vol. 9, no. 866, Sept. 12, 1837)

6. Letter from Santa Fe, August 12, 1837

On August 12, 1837, a caravan of Santa Fe traders left Santa Fe for Missouri. Their departure was hastened by a report the day before that the rebels intended another visit to Santa Fe. The traders had already completed their business, having entered their goods at customs in July and sold them in rented shops or at wholesale to Santa Fe merchants, but this year there had been trouble. Usually a large part of the traders' goods was contraband, hidden from the customs officers in a hundred ingenious ways. The customs officers generally averted their eyes and extended their palms for a bribe, but this year the inspector general had announced an investigation of customs fraud throughout the Republic and the customs officers were not so obliging. Governor Pérez sent Alférez Diego Sáenz and some soldiers to inspect William Workman's goods; the traders armed themselves and resisted the inspection. There was an altercation involving Workman, Patrick Ryder, J. H. Carr, Clifton Boggs, Charles Bent, Josiah Gregg, Elisha Stanley, and others. The traders were indignant, of course, at getting caught at something they consistently got away with, and on July 31 they petitioned the governor, saying that their lives and interests were in danger from the soldiers under Alférez Sáenz, and they demanded punishment of these seditious soldiers who shamelessly attacked them, in spite of the laws of Mexico that guarantee the traders a quiet sojourn in this country as they pursue their lawful commerce. A copy of the petition, made by a clerk unfamiliar with the spelling of foreign names, was signed by Jocias Gregg, Jesse Suttan, Ries Paeteson, Gn. Janett, H. C. Miller, Thos. Rowland, Chas. Bent, J. S. Karn, Jas. Glenday, W. W. Crocesut, J. M. Honiday, I. M. Thonpson, Girsood, W. White, Weingan, Juan Sarlles, Carlos Blumner, Manuel Albares, Rsm. Gittles, and E. Hanley.[1] Among these traders were undoubtedly some who formed the caravan leaving Santa Fe on August 12. Others went south to Mexico; still others, like Carl Blumner, remained in Santa Fe. And one of them probably wrote the following account of the early days of the Río Arriba rebellion, which first appeared in the St. Louis *Republican* of October 2, 1837, and was copied by other newspapers in the United States. Years later, on April 3, 1886, it was reprinted as "an historic document" by the Santa Fe *Daily New Mexican,* a copy of the article having been found by the historian L. Bradford Prince in an unexpected place.

To the Editor of the New Mexican: Flushing, N.Y., March 26.—In looking over a number of old newspapers which had been preserved in my father's house here, I was surprised to find in the "Williamsburg Gazette," of October 14, 1837, the following article on the New Mexican rebellion of that year, and a letter from Santa Fe giving an account of what had occurred down to August 12. Naturally some of the proper names are mis-spelled, but as a contemporary account of the stirring events of those times it is interesting. Yours Truly, L. Bradford Prince.

An Historic Document

Revolution in Santa Fe.—The St. Louis Republican of October 2d, says:—"The early arrival of the Fall Company of Traders from Santa Fe brings advice of a complete revolution in that state. We have been favored by a gentleman of this city, who was formerly concerned in that trade, with an extract from a letter received from his correspondent, giving some of the particulars of the revolution. At the date of these advices, the Americans in the Province had not been molested, although there was no security whatever for property; and the revolutionists, it was said, had marked one of the Americans for sacrifice. This individual, it was observed, would be known when his head was seen upon a pole!"

Santa Fe, Aug. 12, 1837.

Thursday last, the Governor, Don Albino Perez, Political and Military Chief of the territory of New Mexico, accompanied by Abreu, and a small party of soldiers, marched to the Cavada [Cañada] (20 miles from Santa Fe) where a large number of malcontents had assembled, composed of the inhabitants from Rio Arriba to Taos, among whom were the Indians living in the neighborhood, who are partly civilized, and subjects of the general government.

Upon the meeting of the two armies which took place near St. Ildefonso, the Governor ordered his soldiers to fire; at which order all his men went over to the enemy, except 23, of whom one was killed on the spot, and three or four wounded.

The Government [sic] immediately fled, with all who could follow him, to Santa Fe, where they remained until night, under favor of which they started upon good horses in order to get as far as possible from their enemies, who knew how to make more adroit measures to intercept them, for, so soon as they disappeared from the field of battle, they despatched the Indians to cut off their retreat by the Rio Abajo, with orders to spare none of them, which was literally accomplished. The next day the victors encamped at La Chapelle, which is near the town of Santa Fe, and there killed the Governor, Ramon and Marcelino Abreu, Chico Alari, a young lieutenant named Gutieares, and many others, whose names are not known. The triumphant army having declared their leader, Jose Gonzales, an inhabitant of Taos, governor, made the entrance into the town, where he assumed the government, assisted by Rafael Garcia, who commanded the troops with him. All was now tranquil.

But one thing was wanting to complete their purpose—the head of Santiago Abreu, judge of the district—the friend of the stranger and the poor, the talented and meritorious officer, and they received the news that he had been massacred by the Indians of Santo Domingo.

All seems quiet enough at this time, though yesterday the report was that the victors, who had returned home the day after their entrance here, were about to visit us for the purpose of committing further outrages. The new governor, with several others, immediately left here, and we have some assurance that we shall be spared their presence. The country is in a sad and ruinous condition.[2]

1. A. Pérez to Recaudador de Rentas don Ambrocio Armijo, July 24, 1837, MANM roll 23, 617–18; Francisco Sarracino to Gov. Pérez, July 31, 1837, MANM Roll 23, 406–8; petition of

Santa Fe traders to the governor, Aug. 1, 1837, MANM roll 23, 409–10; investigation of the conduct of Alférez Sáenz, undated, with Governor's Papers, MANM roll 23, 622–25.
2. Santa Fe *Daily New Mexican*, April 3, 1886, p. 4, c. 2.

7. Letter of Padre Antonio José Martínez to Bishop Antonio de Zubiría, Taos, September 25, 1837

Padre Antonio José Martínez of Taos is one of the most famous historical figures in New Mexico, and it is surprising that this interesting letter describing his terrifying experiences with the rebels has not already been published. In 1837 Padre Martínez was curate at the "church of El Rancho, Chapel of San Francisco of Assisi," which is, of course, the beautiful and much-photographed church at Ranchos de Taos. Padre Martínez is writing to Bishop Antonio de Zubiría in Durango, and he encloses letters from two other New Mexican priests, Presbítero Don Fernando Ortiz, priest of the Villa de Santa Cruz, dated October 8, 1837, and Padre Juan de Jesús Trujillo of the Albuquerque parish, undated. Ortiz's letter contains material about his troubles with the mob at Santa Cruz, which is used in the text; Trujillo's letter simply repeats what Martínez's letter says and is not used here.

Most Excellent Señor Bishop Don José Antonio de Zubiría.
Taos, September 25, 1837.
My venerated lord of all my esteem.
I must tell you, your excellency, about the occurrences of the present year and why I must beg you that if I have to continue serving in the ecclesiastical ministry, it not be in the curacy of Taos, as I will present explain plainly, and that I am determined to leave promptly for any other place whatever, or remain unemployed in my home.
This is the case: An incident, strange but hardly remote from the turbulent character of the inhabitants of the Villa

of Santa Cruz de la Cañada who have always been the sewage of New Mexico, happened at the end of August: a mob arose in that place, only because one of the Abréus, the prefect, suspended the alcalde of that villa, and the sad consequence was that they killed the governor, Don Alvino Pérez, his secretary, the three Abréus, and others to the number of eighteen, on the eighth, ninth, and tenth of August; but although all the inhabitants of this department were in agreement, for the sake of peace and quiet, that news of the deed would be reported, offering some of them pardon for their actions and awaiting the answer and resolution of the Supreme Government; still all this was not enough but that the same people and my parishioners, the inhabitants of the plaza of San Francisco del Rancho, emulating that which possessed the aforesaid to commit the horrible deed that I imputed to them, although they had conspired they were not the movers, they started a revolution a second time, in order to commit hostilities against those who aided and obeyed the last government, atrocious and wretched purposes touching upon matters of the church; so then I heard something about it, notwithstanding it was kept secret from me, but I had very positive news the second of the month that they were assembling hastily with weapons in order to come and attack my brothers at my house and three other persons of the plaza of San Fernando in opposition to me and to pillage them, so that I could do nothing else but leave, fleeing in the morning of the same day with a brother of mine whom they had persecuted because he was subprefect, and I prepared to go to the city of Santa Fe to be free of this danger, but then when they assumed I would flee, they had me followed, probably with orders to kill me if they caught up with me, which they did not succeed in doing, and so passed the first and second of the month, after which they wrote me proposing that I not be anxious, that I come to my curacy without fear. In view of such an offer I returned in five days along with the governor who had been named, and was well received by the said mob or reunión; it was intimated to me that I had not admitted to a disavowal of the government but in order to afford me rest from certain illnesses caused by the roads and conveyances, it was necessary that they inform the reunión and get permission from the entire reunión, and so I was granted a limit of two days, after which I went to the said place and on the eleventh of the month I was made to appear in a room in which they had a table with the city councilmen around it, and on all sides were rows of men with their weapons ready and lacking only that they were pointed at me: In this way they made me give up the collection of sacramental fees, and the charges for baptisms, marriages and burials; they wanted to eliminate the contributions toward the church building funds, and bury all the dead in the church, to which I said that this was not in my jurisdiction, that if they attempted it by violence and force, I alone could not defend against it, that they would take full responsibility for it and that they themselves would be held responsible to the supreme powers; and they resolved that the church building funds would not be collected and they seized the church of El Rancho, Chapel of San Francisco of Assisi as they had already determined to do, and they buried a corpse by the steps of the chancel and followed this by doing whatever occurred to them which I could not prevent for no less a reason than I was threatened with death if I opposed it; they made me put this cession in writing, and they gave me a similar document for written evidence and for my safety saying that they would take responsibility for burying in the church and that the church funds would not be paid in all of Taos.

As I already knew this matter that they touched upon from previous experience, I told two men, one a city councilman and the other the secretary of the reunión, that doing these things in this way would incur excommunication and inter-diction by the church of this place, and this I believe encouraged them even more to carry out their endeavor and with great stubborness they proceeded: I repeated the same thing to them in the said meeting where I appeared, saying to them that they would not wish to suffer such ecclesiastical punishment, and they said that they would not wish it but that they will not pay obventions nor contributions to church building funds, and that they would be buried in the churches, that for this reason they had made their decree and would continue to support it.

For this, the obventions, church funds and church burial, all the humble people were adamant, with only a few exceptions and those from the sensible people of stature, but of these substantial people the only known conspirators to date are named Córdoba, sons of one Abán Córdoba, deceased, whose two nephews are in jail in Santa Fe because they were those of the first uprising who also had influence in the second, all of them were; one of them being represented among the city councilmen of this place; and so it remains for order to be reestablished as is going to be done in the present time, neither am I determined henceforth to make such collection nor even that of the first fruits [primicias] since they are rejecting that entirely and are determined not to pay them; this is well proved with the example that from then until now, of seven burials, twelve baptisms and four marriages, only one of the married couples has asked me what fees they ought to pay, to whom I told about said cession and that I would receive them only if they were freely offered, and he paid a pledge and offered to pay up what he owed.

Left: Padre Antonio José Martínez. [Ralph Emerson Twitchell, *The History of the Military Occupation of the Terriroty of New Mexico,* (Denver, 1909).]

Church at Ranchos de Taos, Padre Martínez's parish at the time of the rebellion (photo by Wesley Bradfield, Sept., 1917, Museum of New Mexico, #14158).

Interior of the church at Ranchos de Taos, where the rebels horrified
Padre Martínez by burying a corpse at the chancel steps (photo by Paul
A. Wilson, Oct. 22, 1936, Museum of New Mexico #86715).

The last page of the letter of Padre Martínez to Bishop Zubiría dated Taos, September 25, 1837, telling of his treatment by the rebels (Archivo General de la Nación, México, Justicia, Tomo 138, Leg. 48 (1831–1841).

Top: "Descansos" at Chimayó. The crosses mark where a funeral procession stopped to rest on its way to the cemetery; future travelers would also stop here to say a prayer for the deceased. (Taylor Museum, Colorado Springs Fine Arts Center, #2333).

La Garita, where four rebel hostages were shot in January 1838. The road in the foreground was perhaps the same that took Pérez and his little force to meet the rebels at La Mesilla in August 1837 (Rio Grande Collection, Colorado Historical Society).

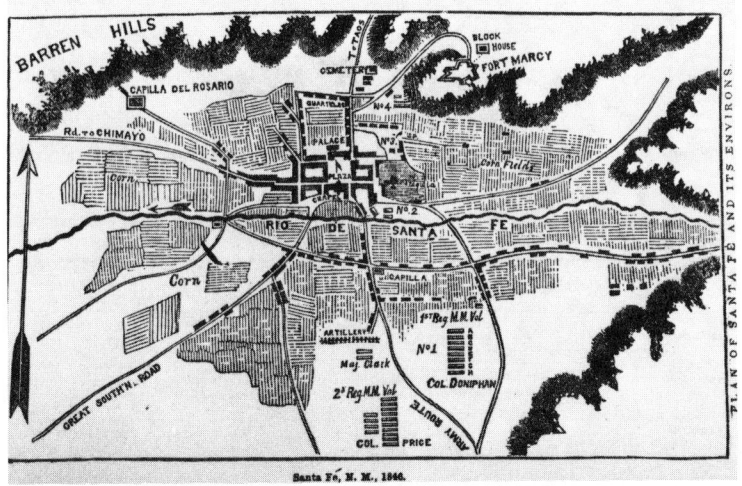

Santa Fe, N. M., 1846.

Except for U.S military installations, Santa Fe of 1846 looked like Santa Fe of 1837–38. The Palace, "Cuarteles" or presidial barracks, Parroquia, Rosario Chapel, "Great South'n Road" (Agua Fría Street) where Pérez was killed, and the cemetery where he was buried, are all recorded in this "Plan" [from John T. Hughes, *Doniphan's Expedition* (1847).] However, the "Rd. to Chimayó" should head northwest rather than west.

PARTE OFICIAL.

GOBIERNO GENERAL.

MINISTERIO DE GUERRA Y MARINA.

Comandancia general del departamento interno del Norte.—Exmo. Sr.—El teniente coronel D. Cayetano Justiniani, con fecha 28 de Agosto próximo pasado, por extraordinario violento me dice lo que sigue.

"Sr. comandante general.—Las adjuntas declaraciones responden á V. S. de la revolucion y desastres causados en el departamento del Nuevo México. Ellas son de tal magnitud, que me obligan á dar conocimiento á V. S. por extraordinario violento, para que impuesta y distribuidas guarcias al del Exmo. Sr. gobernador, puedan V. S. y S. E. dictar del momento las providencias que convengan á salvar y asegurar en adelante de una próxima invasion, que es muy natural intenten desde luego contra el las achivos de aquella, satisfechos de que no tiene alguna fuerza para su defensa, entado V. S. seguro de que si tal fuese emprendida los facciosos antes de reunir las fuerzas que espera, será sacrificado por la parte primera que sucumbe á sus negras ideas, y pues el concepto no son estos que las de los proyistos asesinatos de Tejas.

"Queda tomando mis providencias de defensa, que, aunque débiles, siempre que llegue el caso serán bastantes á dejar bien puesto el nombre de mexicano."

Elévolo á V. E. incluyéndole copias de las declaraciones que se citan, para que se sirva dar cuenta al Exmo. Sr. presidente con tan infausto acontecimiento, manifestándole que para contener males de tanta cuantía se necesitan auxilios de toña cla ses; asegurando á S. E. que entre tanto los recibe, me mantendré á la defensiva, y me prepararé para la ofensiva con los pequeños recursos con que cuento, haciendo, si, todo esfuerzo para mantener la integridad del departamento y el honor del pabellon mexicano en cualquiera caso que se ofrezca.

Dios y libertad, Chihuahua Setiembre 1 de 1837.—A los diez de la noche.—José J. Calvo.—Exmo. Sr. ministro de la guerra y marina.

Comandancia militar del distrito.—En este momento, que serán las siete de la mañana, se me ha dado aviso han llegado del Nuevo Mexico 5 vecinos de esta villa Juan Garces y Guadalupe Miranda, comunicando haberse muerto asesinado todo el pueblo de aquel departamento, dando parte á sus primeras autoridades y á varios individuos respetables, encomendando todos los remedios á su excelencia de que se capaz un pueblo desmoralizado. Hicimandonos las honras V. declaramos á dichos individuos, indagando de ellos el origen de tales desordenes, para poder in que resulte que inmediatamente ocurra al Sr. comandante general de este departamento.

Dios y libertad, Vila del Paso 28 de Agosto de 1837.—Cayetano Justiniani.—Sr. capitan D. Tomás Zuloaga.

El ciudadano Tomás Zuloaga, capitan de la compaña permanente de S. Eleario, y juez nombrado de las presentes diligencias.—Habiendo de nombrar es cribano, segun previenen las ordenanzas generales del ejército, para que actúe en dichas diligencias, que voy á practicar segun la órden que se me ordenó del Sr. prefecto y comandante militar de este distrito, teniente coronel D. Cayetano Justiniani, nombró á Juan Padilla, cabo de la misma compaña, para que ejerza el empleo de escribano; y habiéndole advertido de la obligacion que contrae, acepta, para y protesta guardar aguu y fidelidad en cuanto accion; y para que conste lo firmo conmigo en la villa del Paso, á los veintiocho dias del mes de Agosto de 1837.—Tomás Zuloaga.—Juan Padilla.

Incontinente, el mismo Sr. juez fiscal hizo comparecer ante sí á D. Juan Garcia, vecino de esta villa, que acaba de arribar del departamento del Nuevo Mexico, á quien ante mí el presente escribano hizo levantar la mano derecha; y preguntado prometió decir la verdad sobre el punto de que es voy á interrogar? Dijo que sí. Preguntado su nombre, empleo, y estado? Respondió llamarse Juan Garcia, vecino, labrador de esta misma vila, y que llegó al amanecer de este dia. Preguntado si sabe que recientemente han acaecido en el departamento del Nuevo Mexico acerca de una conspiracion que aquellos pueblos han ejecutado contra sus autoridades, que origen han tenido estos desórdenes, con que miras se han dirigido, que personas han tenido por mano de los facciosos, y qué es mas menudamente cuando sepa acerca del particular. Dijo: Que hallandose el que declara en la capital del departamento de Nuevo Mexico con miras mercantiles el dia 3 del corriente mes, supo por algunos vecinos, y aun por la voz pública, que los pueblos

In this copy of the *Diario del Gobierno de la República Mexicana,* Justiniani's interrogation of the Santa Fe traders at El Paso was published, giving Mexico its first news of the rebellion (courtesy of the Bancroft Library, University of California, Berkeley).

One of several copies of a portrait of Manuel Armijo drawn by Alfred S. Waugh in 1846 in full uniform of a Mexican general. Armijo said that Waugh's drawing of him was the only likeness ever taken [*Travels in Search of the Elephant*, ed. John Francis McDermott (St. Louis, 1951, p. 134] (Museum of New Mexico).

Manuel Armijo's house on the plaza at Albuquerque (Whitford Collection, Colorado Historical Society).

Donaciano Vigil (McNitt Collection, State Records Center and Archives, Santa Fe #6547).

That will be enough explanation for your excellency to understand what occurred, and I omit to refer to other details in all their particulars that touch in a heretical difficulty which I have been unable to avoid with politeness, benevolence, exhortation and other means for which those who have been my parishioners ought to be very grateful to me, but everything has been in vain and I have barely escaped with my life and my few patrimonial goods of which I still do not feel secure. What I seek in sending your excellency this information is what you may decide for me in another letter.

Our Lord guard the important life of your excellency as desires your affectionate son and therefore your servant who kisses your hand.

Antonio José Martínez [rubric]

(Archivo General de la Nación [México], Justicia, tomo 138, legajo 48 (183–41), 166–68; copies in the Bancroft Library, Berkeley, California)

8. Letter of Manuel Armijo, October 11, 1837

On October 11, 1837, Provisional Governor Manuel Armijo wrote the following letter describing events in New Mexico from the pronouncement at Tomé to the treaty with the rebels. The letter is written in Manuel Armijo's natural style (as opposed to what Kendall calls his "high-sounding fanfaronade style"). In either its natural or high-sounding phase, Armijo's writing style is a tangle of dependent clauses and interminable sentences, which I have retained in my translation except where comprehension is threatened. Although the letter, like its author, is not overly modest, neither is it the "highly colored account of his own exploits" described by both Kendall and Gregg. The letter, in fact, shows Manuel Armijo at his best—decisive, commanding, straightforward, perceptive, generous to his cohorts.

Official report./General Government./Minister of War and Navy./Provisional Government of New Mexico.—Most Excellent Sir.—

This department has been involved in the horrors of a disastrous and barbarous revolution into which perverse men led it, setting the people against the constitutional laws and government that rule us; after they committed in their exhilaration every kind of crime, impiously assassinating persons of the highest offices, and when they were preparing another bloody explosion even more dangerous, having for its only object general desolation and ruin, on the eighth of September last I pronounced in Tomé for order, constitution and laws, as I had the honor of informing you by extraordinario dated Bernalillo on the 13th of the same, where I had stopped on my way to this city with the liberating force I had assembled, at the mercy of the many [line of type lost] . . . or to be victims of the furor of a disordered insurrection that had no other destination and took no other path than killing and robbing.

Now that I am able to do it, I have the satisfaction of giving to the most excellent president through you an account of the happy and perhaps unexpected outcome of my dangerous undertaking, in which without the bloodshed that seemed inevitable, I succeeded in putting down the revolution, establishing order and obedience to desecrated laws and to the supreme government of the nation which was necessary to do in order to succeed, and I will tell you also about the present situation in the department, exposed to being lost if opportune, prompt, and efficient remedy had not been applied.

On the 14th of September, as soon as I arrived in this capital where the worthy permanent company, which had been disbanded, again took up arms along with the citizenry with the greatest enthusiasm for repelling the cantonment of rebels who were expected any moment, I was recognized as commander in chief of all the troops, with the rank of colonel of the liberating army, according to the copy of the commission (document no. 1) and acknowledgement of the act (document no. 2). The forces at my command were a thousand-odd men, whom I trained in the management of arms, for as citizens they knew almost nothing about it, and I saw to the mounting of artillery, repair of broken arms, and reinforcement of supplies, expecting also to enter into communications with the Cantón of rebels, now approaching, before fighting them, inasmuch as their force, numbering three thousand men, was considerable, and their position on high ground very advantageous, my object being to avoid battle and the loss of Mexican blood if possible, for I knew that most of the mob had been deceived in their ignorance by false promises, and that others of them had joined out of fear of the rebel force. I took the opportunity of having the commander of the Cantón, Don Pablo Montoya, direct a letter to Governor Gonzales (elected by the same factions) who had already been arrested in Santa Fe, explaining the factitious causes of this new uprising (document no. 3); I invited him to make a verbal treaty (document no. 4) to which he acceded after various arguments (documents nos. 5 through 11) coming at last to this city with all the city councilmen and their alternates from that Cantón which remained a league and a half distant from here while I was preparing to march on them.

It was necessary to receive these men in the manner that had been offered to them, and to use them with all the prudence necessary for success in the undertaking, without loosing the torrents of blood they were prepared to shed, and as I used the greatest persuasion in conjunction with an energetic decision to fight them, it resulted in the drafting of terms of agreement (document no. 12) by which they were obliged to dissolve their Cantón, declare their government and laws invalid, and subject themselves to my orders, giving me the position of superior head of both political and military commands until the resolution of His Excellency the president of the republic, and although there were various difficulties and debates before they would comply with the first two conditions, these difficulties contributed to the achievement of the rest of the conditions so that at last they were satisfied with the total dissolution of their reunión and the arrest of the delinquents (document no. 13), who were indicted in order to receive the punishment imposed by law for their enormous crime.

In this manner concluded a revolution that presented a most horrible aspect of misfortunes so frequent and so great that they filled the inhabitants of this soil with confusion, having no other recourse but to succumb, for fear of the terrifying army they saw committing crimes with the most outrageous cruelty. In fact, the way they killed the governor, Colonel Don Albino Pérez, district judge Don Santiago Abréu, prefect Don Ramón Abréu, secretary of government Don Jesús María [sic], Lieutenant Don Joaquín Hurtado, Alférez Don Diego Sáenz, Don Miguel Sena and others, cannot be described without the consternation humanity feels in the highest degree, being better, then, to omit the circumstances of such horrendous assassinations, even more criminal than merely having deprived the victims of life. One feels surprise and fear to know that these evildoers, with the show of authority that they pleased to put on, invited the barbarous nations that surround this department to form an allegiance against the supreme government, and to help by cutting off communication with the interior of the republic, counting as well on the Pueblo Indian people whom as a weak, credulous, ignorant people very addicted to the sack and spoils of war, they easily seduced, persuading them that the departmental laws would take from them a third part of the fruits of their labor, taxing heavily the common benefits of water, wood, pastures, and even their own children and wives.

The aim of the factions was, as is evident, to remain independent of the government of the Mexican nation; to put an end to every person who has an average education; to be governed by no established law, which was their excuse for sentencing all the archives to the flames; to destroy fortunes in a general sack; and to live without subjection to any precept or authority, identifying themselves with the savage tribes and putting themselves on the same level, making the same cause with their same interests.

There is no doubt but that the Mexican nation would have lost, perhaps forever, this integral part of its territory had not some of its people taken a strong stand, seized the right opportunity, and shown great fortitude; but it is even more doubtful that this would have succeeded had not the supreme government extended its protecting hand to this unfortunate territory, providing the help required to quell the rebellion without much difficulty. To make this department happy and to protect it from the dangers surrounding it, all that would be required is funds to support three veteran companies, with commanders capable of maintaining discipline. But for now, to assure the present tranquility of the department and to prevent a revolution such as it has suffered and which produced such exaltation in the people as to predispose them to form another revolution, I have sought from the commanding general of Chihuahua at least two hundred guns, as I wrote in my previous letter and now repeat as of the highest importance and most imperious need in this precarious and difficult situation, in which the only thing that quiets the conspirators and delays another rebellion is the fear of troops coming from afar to punish the rebel leaders and show that the supreme government intends to vindicate its laws and is not insolvent, as the conspirators supposed. With this object I beg the said commanding general to send quickly the resources to obtain immediate help, without which I am certain we will return to battle, and I do not know what will happen to this department.

Before concluding this statement, I must do justice to the heroic patriotism and notable services of the gentlemen who promoted the pronouncement of Tomé and worked constantly without sparing personal means or sacrifice, recommending first as worthy of the consideration of His Excellency the president the intrepid priest Don Francisco Ignacio de Madariaga, curate of Tomé, who inspired the idea and in my company raised the glorious cry of order and laws when no one dared to breathe and when it appeared foolhardy even to imagine it, placing himself beside the liberating army as its chaplain; Don Vicente Sánchez Vergara, secretary of the same army who originally influenced the formation of the troop at Santa Fe, helping to outfit it and at the same time sending secret communications to Río Abajo, taking a very considerable part in the pronouncement and in its happy outcome, risking his life to connect this capital with the liberating forces; Don Mariano Chávez y Castillo, lieutenant colonel of the same liberating army; Don Antonio Sandoval, Don Pedro José Perea, Don Juan Perea, Don Vicente Otero, Don Juan Otero, and Don Santiago Ulibarrí whose influence supported the undertaking in the highest degree, subscribing heavily towards the expenses and also taking up arms as soldiers; the gentlemen Don Juan Estevan Pino and Don Juan Rafael Ortiz, who cooperated in the same manner, advancing themselves alone the succor for the company; the captains of militia, Don Juan Cristóbal Armijo, Don José Salazar, Don José Antonio Chávez, and Lieutenant Don Ramón Aragón for the enthusiasm and valor with which they served the army; alférez of the active militia Don Julián Armijo, Alcaldes Don Francisco Ortiz y Delgado, Don Ambrosio Armijo, and Don José Felipe Castillo, who above others of their class gave evidence of adhesion to the cause of order; the interim curate of this capital Don José Francisco Leyba, so enthusiastic in the cause of order that he offered to confer with the rebels, which was too dangerous considering the class of people composing that reunión; and finally recommending with singular distinction the worthy troop of this city which gathered simultaneously and voluntarily to take up arms to sustain order, in spite of the opposition of Assistant Inspector Lieutenant Colonel Don José María Ronquillo, who resigned his command and retreated with demonstrations of fear and cowardice to El Paso del Norte; I commend as well the officers of this garrison Captain Don José Caballero, Lieutenant Don José Silva, Lieutenant Don José Hernández, Alféreces Don Francisco Martínez, Don Esquipulas Caballero, Don Rafael Tapia, Don Ramón Baca, and Don Manuel Ramírez.

In sending you this pleasant communication, begging you to bring it to the superior knowledge of the most excellent president, I have the honor to protest to you the assurances of my high consideration and respect.

God and Liberty. Santa Fe October 11, 1837.

Manuel Armijo
Most excellent minister of war and navy.

(*Diario del Gobierno de la república Mexicana*, vol. 9, no. 945, Nov. 30, 1837, pp. 361–62)

9. Proclamation of Manuel Armijo, January 7, 1838(?)

Manuel Armijo probably issued this proclamation on January 7, 1838, although the document remaining in the New Mexican Archives is undated. The purpose of the proclamation was to announce that he had received the appointment of governor and principal commandant of arms, and to transmit the president's message, which was that he had appointed Armijo to support the new departmental plan adopted by the nation, and to bring the people of New Mexico to order. The proclamation starts quietly enough, but then Armijo works up to his most elaborate "fanfaronade" style. The proclamation is more than a political speech, however; this and Armijo's other speeches presented here contain his opinions and principles about governing New Mexico, which directed his actions throughout his years as governor—his terror of anarchy and his attachment to law and order, truth and justice, and especially to peace achieved not through battle but negotiation, and maintained at all costs, even loss of honor.

Manuel Armijo, Constitutional Governor and Principal Commandant of Arms in the Department of New Mexico, to its inhabitants:

Fellow citizens: The supreme government with knowledge

of the terrible events that befell this department in consequence of the revolutionary movement at the beginning of last August against the authorities and constitutional laws, is pleased to name me governor and principal commandant of arms with the intention of putting into practice public administration conforming to the system adopted by the nation, which the president immediately took the most active measures to sustain and enforce; at the same time he desires conclusively, without the need of further discussion, that the people, misled by the deceit and malevolence of some ambitious and unnatural types, might return to order. Enough time has now passed since these horrible events; enough actions have been experienced to give the most gullible souls knowledge of the iniquitous designs of the revolution, its chimerical roots and ensnaring net; and more, that the misfortunes in which the department is involved are sufficient so that all the people and especially the honorable and hardworking citizens who are strongly desirous of peace, are conscious in the extreme of the horrendous crime committed by these tumultuous factions that proclaim anarchy, ruin, and desolation, shattering the national unity to which we are tied in sweet obedience to a free, paternal, and magnanimous government which fortunately leads us; also as fraud and deceit can never prevail against truth and justice, the people ought to be undeceived of error and be certain that the constitutional laws that raised this territory to the rank of department, which puts it equal in pleasures and rights with the rest of the republic, instead of imposing those contributions and taxes that maliciously and falsely were attributed to them in order to discredit them and thus realize atrocious vengeance by this means, to satisfy villainous and invidious passions working for private interest; so I repeat, such taxes being authorized by law positively prohibit abuses in this matter, being a particular attribution of the only supreme legislative power that has the faculty of doing so when the necessities of the country demand it. It can be expected that there will be many taught and marked by public opinion, agents and vile promoters of such evils to whom the candor, innocent credulity, and patriotism that forms the general character of these naturally peaceful people, will make themselves known with terrifying surprise, despising the stupid seductions with which they are precipitated into the abyss of the lowest of most lamentable crimes, to the general disrepute and to the execration of the entire world! Miserable ones, they are unworthy of living among men and of what shelters the country in her maternal womb! The knife of the law will cut off the criminal heads and make an example of just severity of those who imitate such detestable conduct! It will not be surprising that in the beginning this government will be put in possession of the legitimate authorities, such as the prefects, subprefects, and justices of the peace, and start the investigation of those perverse criminals who have expressed the wish to raise again with deceit the temper of the people, that they may thus procure impunity for their crimes, or that others may be joined with them, and be lost; then evil to many is consolation of fools, according to the popular axiom; but as I have said, they cannot succeed in spite of their attempts because it is not easy to deceive the people often, whose spirit is always that of tranquility, and whose interest and individual security lie in peace, in government, and in laws that alone look to the common happiness. Therefore my operations as governor ought to be public, frank, and accompanied by the rectitude proper to justice. I do not doubt that a happy outcome will result, in certain knowledge that not for lack of energy and resolution will the truly delinquent ever be without the merited punishment that the laws determine, likewise the innocent without the protection that the laws provide. The supreme government has put at my disposition enough forces to operate in the proposed event; but the advantage of reason and sad experience is a force more powerful for us—we need no other, so that only in the last extreme will we use arms. Your fellow citizen and friend.

(MANM, r. 23, fr. 646–48)

10. Circular of Manuel Armijo, January 19, 1838

The following circular of Manuel Armijo, dated January 19, 1838, begins with news of the rebel movement under Antonio Vigil at Truchas, and concludes with a strong warning to the "poor Ignorant Indian who knows not what he does."

The citizen Manuel Armijo, constitutional governor and principal commandant of arms of the department of New Mexico.

I have just received official news from the municipal council of the villa of La Cañada that the revolutionary, Antonio Vigil, has formed another revolution in the district of Truchas, and that he has already stirred up a number of people. These unhappy ones, worthy of compassion, will be promptly reduced to order by national troops, but as a government interested in the public prosperity, I have to watch that the evils do not increase, and see to it that the wicked do not deceive the people, making them commit crimes and leading them to their ruin. I want the Indians of the country to know that my aim is none other than to sustain the law, punishing only the truly culpable, protecting the ignorant even when they have cooperated with previous revolutions, having been motivated by the seductions and deceits of the promoters. I want them to suffer no hostile treatment however light, nor especially do I want their poor families to suffer the terrible scourge of war to which they are provoked by the rebels of Las Truchas at those *reuniones,* as criminal as they are insignificant, so that they forget the clemency and commiseration they have enjoyed until now; but once they are freed from their obstinacy and backsliding, one must work in another manner, and therefore I am convinced that the blame always falls on the poor ignorant Indian who knows not what he does. I am warning them, so that they may not be deceived, so that they may close their ears to the invitations, and so that they may live in peace in the confidence that the government values them, but if in spite of this they take part in the revolution, they may not afterwards complain nor plead ignorance, for then the rigor of the law will fall equally on everyone.

Santa Fe, January 19, 1838
[rubric]

(MANM r. 24, fr. 1314–15)

11. Circular of Manuel Armijo, January 24, 1838

Manuel Armijo's circular of January 24, 1938, announces the decapitation of the hostages, with a paragraph of "fanfaronade" justifying their deaths, and the promise that Armijo's government will do its duty without considerations of friendship or interest.

Circular. Today at nine in the morning the traitorous criminals of this nation, Juan José Esquibel, Juan Vigil, Deciderio Montoya, and Antonio Abad Montoya, were decapitated. They were the authors and ringleaders of the frightful conspiracy of the Villa of La Cañada which scandalously threatened the national unity, the sovereignty of the laws that constitute the government, and the persons that represent it in the highest positions of this department, whom they assassinated with an impiety without example. These wretches, primordial instruments of such horrendous crimes, were being judged under the formulas and specific covenants that the law prescribes; but the public tranquility is menaced by a new uprising of the perfidious Antonio Vigil who has convoked tumultuously the unhappy people of La Cañada and Chimayó into sustaining the revolution, dishonoring the government with the greatest insults and threatening it by taking by force the expressed criminals, whose execution was violent and a well-deserved punishment for their atrocious crime.

The just heaven cries out for this execution, and the same guilt deserves its consequent effects. The government proposes to do its duty with energetic measures, without respect to the individual, nor considerations of friendship or interest, this will be the fixed rule of its conduct. God grant that this spectacle so sad for peaceful New Mexico may be the last to appear to its natural humanity and good feeling. I bring this to your knowledge so that you may publish it in your jurisdiction.

(MANM r. 24, fr. 1325–26)

12. Décimas

Décimas are popular ballads with stanzas of ten octosyllabic lines. In the absence of newspapers and novels, décimas served to disseminate the news and to tell stories. Even inexperienced singers could memorize the poems easily, and as a result many have survived until the present. Parts of three décimas are presented here, two remembered by Rafael Chacón, a child of four at the time of the rebellion, and one collected by John Donald Robb in 1945 from an elderly singer of Bernalillo, New Mexico. The first two décimas are from the translation of the "Memoirs" of Major Rafael Chacón, completed in 1912. Chacón writes of these old ballads that "their swing and rhythm come back to my mind like a wail of the past."

> And the treacherous deceivers
> From the Villa de la Cañada
> Committed a thousand crimes
> Born of their guilty conscience.
>
> These men of the braided hair
> Framed up their conspiracy
> Rafael García and El Chopón
> Came to the front in a hurry
>
> Then they started a war dance
> Among them, these two bullies,
> And of all who formed the Cantón
> These two worthies were the worst.
>
> . . . The people again come out
> With great excitement and noise
> Because victory has perched
> With the alcalde of La Cañada;
>
> And because they are such boors
> That they cannot even write
> They have appointed as secretary
> Don Donaciano Vigil.

The second décima was also recollected by Major Rafael Chacón. There is information here for the historian about feelings toward the rebels, whom the poem calls rustics, half-breeds, fools, men of greed, ignorance, and ambition, with evil dispositions. The poem contrasts the "clean and honorable weapons" of the noble military with the arrows of the ignoble rebels, and deplores the clemency shown the hostages because of "little children crying."

> Insurgent Chimayoses
> Men of the plaided coats
> Who have abandoned the looms
> To rebel against the country.
> By sedition of the Half-breed
> They have started a rebellion,
> Seeking to destroy the laws
> Of our constitution;
> Rustics and without attainments,
> They did not seek the observance
> Of the laws of the Department,
> They have provoked a rude shock
> With the military forces.
> None of them have stood their ground,
> All ran away in great haste,
> But many have found it bitter,
> This sedition of the Half-breed,
> The men who had been their leaders
> Died at the hands of the soldiers,
> Many, and also Gonzales,
> For their greed and their ambition;
> And their evil dispositions
> Added to their other crimes,
> And the little children crying
> Have obtained for themselves clemency.
> It was your ignorance, brothers,
> That has caused us this rebellion.
> What noble thing is the military,

Clean and honorable weapons,
Which they sought to meet with arrows,
This aggregation of rustics.
Oh, the thoughts of these poor fools,
They sought to undo the laws,
Vigil was the biggest traitor,
Thinking to derive advantage,
Because by sheer abuse
He though to save the Montoyas,
Because his understanding failed him,
He being of a wicked heart,
Overriding all the laws
Of our constitution, [1]

The third décima about the rebellion is quoted in both Major
Chacón's "Memoirs" and John Donald Robb's book, *Hispanic
Folk Music of New Mexico and the Southwest: A Self-Portrait
of a People*. I have quoted the first portion of Dr. Robb's
translation, which is divided into traditional décima stanzas.

Planta

In the ill-fated year of
Eighteen hundred thirty-seven,
Unlucky New Mexico,
What has happened to us?

I

The district judge has died,
The prefect, and the sheriff also,
And thus no one complains
When a crime is committed.
I have observed
When the innocent man paid,
And how the people suffer

These great torments;
They will always remember you,
Year of eighteen hundred.

II

The state's committee [*junta departmental*]
Convened by necessity
And had to consider
The wicked violations of law;
Who will stand in the presence
Of that Supreme Court?
Who will be the one without fear,
To speak for their territory
Seeing the vengeance, the hate,
Of that which has happened to us?
I wish that I had not seen you,
Ill-fated thirty-seven.[2]

1. Both these décimas are from a copy of Rafael Chacon's "Memoirs" in the Western Historical Collections of Norlin Library, University of Colorado, Boulder, Colorado. I am deeply indebted to Dr. David Sandoval of the University of Southern Colorado for calling this valuable source to my attention.
2. (Norman: University of Oklahoma Press, 1980), p. 408. Dr. Robb's book has an entire section on décimas, with an introduction explaining the structure of the poems and a transcription of the melody, which in New Mexico was the same for all décimas (pp. 376–417).

13. Excerpt from Carlos María Bustamante, *El Gabinete Mexicano* . . . [1842]

Carlos María Bustamante took part in the struggle for Mexican independence and was for many years the deputy from Oaxaca to the national congress. He was a great admirer of

Manuel Armijo, and dedicated a book to him after Armijo's capture of the invading Texans, in 1841. H. H. Bancroft devotes six pages of small print to Bustamante's adventurous career and to a critical analysis of his writings, concluding that Bustamante is biased and not sufficiently discriminating in his use of sources (*History of Mexico*, vol. 5 in *The Works of Hubert Howe Bancroft*, vol. 13 [San Francisco, 1885], pp. 802–8.) Bustamante's account of the rebellion is drawn from letters of participants, eyewitnesses, and Armijo himself; its description of the battle of the puerto or puertocito of Poajoaque is the best account we have.

Letter III

Revolution of New Mexico on the 9th of August, 1837
Mexico, February 6, 1841
My dear friend.—In the session of the 11th of September an official letter of the commander of Chihuahua gave an account to congress of a very bloody insurrection in New Mexico in which died the military commandant, Don Alvino Pérez, the departmental assembly, the district judge, and other principal persons. These misfortunes were described more fully in the declarations taken by Cayetano Justiniani, commander of El Paso del Norte, from various citizens of that villa who had arrived from New Mexico and had heard of, or were eyewitness to, that catastrophe. I gather from this that the rebels collected in the Villa of Santa Cruz de la Cañada. The commander Pérez went out to fight them with more than a hundred men and a cannon. Scarcely had the enemy been sighted than his own soldiers treasonously passed over to the rebels and charged them fiercely until he had to flee with twenty-five men, and they reached the mesa of Santo Domingo where he was killed after selling his life very dearly, for in spite of being disarmed of his pistols and saber,

he defended himself gallantly with a dagger; they cut off his head, carried it off and threw it in the principal plaza. Don José María Ronquillo who had succeeded him in command went out with a white flag to meet the factions and to offer them his services. That is all that is now known about the revolution. On October 12, by a letter from New Mexico, we are assured that the department is restored to order. The revolution was caused by a part of the North American caravan bringing much merchandise, the duties on which the Anglo-Americans did not wish to pay, and the governor in trying to force them to exhibit their goods, provoked them to rebellion.[1]

Events were not made clear until the 30th of November through an official letter sent to the government by Don Manuel Armijo, a leader that posterity will see as a benefactor of New Mexicans. He pronounced for order in the town of Tomé and through his prudence and valor succeeded in suffocating a rebellion that will go down in history as most barbarous and disastrous.

As soon as he arrived in Santa Fe, the permanent company was reunited with the citizens to attack the rebels who remained in their district, and he was recognized as commander in chief of this little force, with the title of colonel. He devoted himself to disciplining the men, putting together the artillery and providing ammunition. Meanwhile the rebels, numbering three thousand advantageously situated, were preparing to fight; but he entered into communication with their chief, Don José Gonzales, and other officers of the Cantón, and with prudence succeeded in convincing them to recognize the authority of the government, to dissolve and subject themselves to his orders, giving him the double character of military and political chief, delivering to him, moreover, the leaders of the uprising. In this way the uprising ended *for the time being,* and avoided the total loss of the country, for the rebels had decided to ally themselves with the wild Indian nations surrounding them and to destroy everything, preferring to live the wandering life of the savages.

Armijo doubted, and with reason, the sincerity and duration of this treaty; but in order to secure it he sought arms and effective aid from the general command of Chihuahua. His modesty was such that he admitted to the government that the author of the project of putting down the rebellion was the curate of Tomé Don Francisco Ignacio Madariaga, from whom went out the first voice of reason when none dared to breathe and it appeared rash even to imagine it.[2] Time showed that Armijo was not mistaken in his conjectures, for the enemies of peace returned to their revolutionary ideas, alarmed most of the inhabitants of Santa Fe and the Indian pueblos, formed a new encampment at the Villa which was augmented daily by those who showed themselves to be more insolent and wild every day. It was therefore decided to fight them, running the risk of meeting the same fate as his unfortunate predecessor and companions. Commander Justiniani of El Paso del Norte, who from the beginning had shown the energy and skill of a competent soldier, arrived with a section of 296 men and ceded the command to Armijo, even though he was the senior officer and Armijo was a civilian. Both forces together numbered 582 men, and marched upon more than 1,300 rebels at the Puerto de Pojoaque, seven leagues distant from Santa Fe. The rebels were situated advantageously on the heights and crags looming above Armijo, making this point difficult to take and much more so because of the snow that covered it. Availing themselves of this advantage the enemy began to fire from the shelter of a breastwork, and tried to flank our forces in considerable groups; but Justiniani deployed the Veracruz squadron in battle, and using the other forces in pickets and guerrillas, put the enemy to flight, and before a quarter of an hour they had captured that place. A small force pursued the enemy, which lay in ambush in a breastwork situated in advantageous terrain where a second action was undertaken in which four Veracruz dragoons died and others were wounded; but the factions were evicted from this point. In the first action Antonio Vigil, enemy commander, died, four prisoners were taken, and twenty were left dead, not counting the seriously wounded. Then Armijo entered the Villa of La Cañada without opposition, with which the rebellion ended. This brilliant and decisive action took place on the 27th of January, 1838, a cruelly cold day. The supreme government rewarded these important services, conferring on Armijo the rank of army colonel and the office of governor. How wonderful it is that in such conflicts and circumstances an obscure man usually comes forth to reestablish the dignity of the laws. Such is the order of Providence! . . .

(Carlos María Bustamante, *El Gabinete Mexicano durante el segundo periodo de la administración del Exmo. Señor Presidente D. Anastasio Bustamante hasta la entrega del mando al Exmo. Señor Presidente interino D. Antonio López de Santa-Anna, y continuación del cuadro histórico de la Revolución Mexicana.* México: Jose M. Lara, 1842, vol. 1, pp. 33–35)

1. [Bustamante's note]: Later events that we refer to in their place confirmed this report, that the Anglo-Americans came to conquer New Mexico in a formal expedition, all of whom were made prisoners of the government.

2. [Bustamante's note]: These are his words, this letter is dated October 11.

Notes

1. For fear of American invasion, see Antonio Barreiro, *Supplement* [1832] in H. Bailey Carroll and J. Villasana Haggard, eds. *Three New Mexico Chronicles* (Albuquerque: The Quivira Society, 1942), p. 75; letter of Comandante Militar of New Mexico to Comandante General of Chihuahua #56, Sept. 16, 1836, Mexican Archives of New Mexico (hereinafter cited as MANM), microfilm publication of the New Mexico State Records Center and Archives, roll 19, frames 679–80; and report of Antonio José Martínez to General Santa Anna, Nov. 28, 1843, translated and quoted in William A. Keleher, *Turmoil in New Mexico* (Santa Fe: Rydal Press, 1952), p. 67. For Texan designs on New Mexico, see Act of December 19, 1836, *Laws of the Republic of Texas,* I, 133; inaugural address of Mirabeau B. Lamar, 1836, in Joseph Milton Nance, *After San Jacinto: The Texas-Mexican Frontier, 1836–1841* (Austin: University of Texas Press, 1963), p. 102; and letter of Deputy Juan Felipe Ortiz to Governor, Dec. 19, 1837, MANM r. 23, fr. 501–3. For Navajos, see letter of Governor Manuel Armijo to Comandante General, Chihuahua, Feb. 5, 1838, MANM r. 24, fr. 1243–44. For Apache depredations, see letter of Governor of New Mexico to Ministerio de Relaciones, Aug. 31, 1832, MANM r. 18, fr. 296; letter of Comandante Principal of New Mexico to Comandante General of Chihuahua, March 5, 1836, MANM, r. 19, fr. 667–69.

2. Eleanor B. Adams and Fray Angélico Chávez, eds., *The Missions of New Mexico, 1776: A Description by Fray Francisco*

Atanasio Domínguez with Other Contemporary Documents (Albu-
querque: University of New Mexico Press, 1956), pp. 82–83; Josiah
Gregg, *Commerce of the Prairies,* ed. Max L. Moorhead (Norman:
University of Oklahoma Press, 1954), pp. 98–114.

3. In 1824 La Cañada had a population of 5,743 (MANM
r. 4, fr. 148), about six hundred more than Santa Fe had in 1827
(Carroll and Haggard, *Three New Mexico Chronicles,* p. 88). By
1845 Santa Cruz de la Cañada had only 2,135 souls (MANM r.
40, fr. 509).

4. For "Chimayó Rebellion" see "An Account of the Chimayó Rebellion, 1837" (document 3). For "Chimayosos," plaided
coats, braided hair, and "rustics," see *décima* quoted in "Memories
of Rafael Chacón" (document 12); for *jerga* see E. Boyd, *Popular
Arts of Spanish New Mexico* (Santa Fe; Museum of New Mexico
Press, 1974), pp. 181–87.

5. Ward A. Minge, "Frontier Problems in New Mexico Pre-
ceding the Mexican War, 1840–1846," Ph.D. dissertation, University of New Mexico, 1965, p. 96, shows that there were twenty
Indian Pueblos in New Mexico with a combined population of
8,700 in 1821 and 7,600 in 1850. For a contemporary's description of the Pueblo Indians, see Gregg, *Commerce of the Prairies,*
p. 195.

6. For social organization of Río Arriba, see John R. Van
Ness, "Hispanic Village Organization in Northern New Mexico,"
in *The Survival of Spanish American Villages,* ed. Paul Kutsche,
(Colorado College Studies, no. 15: spring 1979), pp. 31–44; for
genízaros, see Robert Archibald, "Acculturation and Assimilation
in Colonial New Mexico," *New Mexico Historical Review* 53 (July
1978); for Americans in the Taos Valley in 1841, see letter of
Charles Bent to Manuel Álvarez, Taos, Jan. 30, 1841, Álvarez
Papers, New Mexico State Records Center and Archives, Santa
Fe; for Americans on the Arkansas see Janet Lecompte, *Pueblo,
Hardscrabble, Greenhorn: The Upper Arkansas, 1832–1846* (Norman: University of Oklahoma Press, 1978). Manuel Armijo's census of 1840 gives the first district (Río Arriba) 33,824 souls, and

the second district (Río Abajo) 21,579 souls (Carroll and Haggard, *Three New Mexico Chronicles*, p. 89).

7. Gregg, *Commerce of the Prairies*, pp. 203–4, 268–77; Max L. Moorhead, *New Mexico's Royal Road* (Norman: University of Oklahoma Press, 1954), pp. 109–16.

8. For commerce, see Carroll and Haggard, *Three New Mexico Chronicles*, pp. 35–43, 106–7 and Moorhead, *New Mexico's Royal Road*, pp. 28–75; for peons, see Gregg, *Commerce of the Prairies*, p. 166, and James Josiah Webb, *Adventures in the Santa Fe Trade, 1844–1847*, ed. Ralph P. Bieber, The Southwest Historical Series, vol. 1 (Glendale, Cal.: Arthur H. Clark, 1931), pp. 101–4; for rebel pueblos of Río Abajo, see testimony of Guadalupe Miranda, Aug. 28, 1837 (document 5).

9. The author of "An Account of the Chimayó Rebellion, 1837" was probably Albino Chacón (see document 3). For a short history of Republican Mexico, see Henry Bamford Parkes, *A History of Mexico* (Boston: Houghton Mifflin, 1969; original edition 1938). Michael P. Costeloe, *La primera república federal de México (1824–1835)*, p. 454, gives the terms of presidents to 1835.

10. Deprivations of New Mexican life are described in Pino's *Exposición* and Barreiro's *Supplement*, in Carroll and Haggard, *Three New Mexico Chronicles*, pp. 35–104 and in Gregg, *Commerce of the Prairies*, pp. 103–85.

11. Marta Weigle, *Brothers of Light, Brothers of Blood: The Penitentes of the Southwest* (Albuquerque: University of New Mexico Press, 1976), pp. 24–5, 45, 51.

12. Letter of Armijo to Comandante General, Chihuahua, Feb. 5, 1838, MANM r. 24, fr. 1243–44.

13. Alfred Barnaby Thomas, *Forgotten Frontiers: A Study of the Spanish Indian Policy of Don Juan Bautista de Anza, Governor of New Mexico, 1777–1787* (Norman: University of Oklahoma Press, 1932), pp. 47–83.

14. Pino, *Exposición* (1812), states that the veteran company had 121 men; Barreiro, *Supplement*, says it had 106 men; both in Carroll and Haggard, *Three New Mexico Chronicles*. By October 1835, the troop had only 60 men, who were dismissed for lack of

money to support them (Comandante Militar of New Mexico to Comandante Principal of Chihuahua, Oct. 15, 1835, MANM r. 19, fr. 646–48); on Aug. 1, 1837, the 78 men of the troop were again retired to their houses ("Lista y extracto de revista," Aug. 1, 1837, MANM 4. 24, fr. 47–50). For the troop function, see Comandante Militar to Comandante Principal, Oct. 15, 1835, cited; for Santa Anna's order see Tornel, Secretaría de Guerra y Marina, to Comandante Principal, New Mexico, Dec. 11, 1835, MANM r. 19, fr. 370.

15. Comandante Militar of New Mexico to Comandante General of Chihuahua, Feb. 5, 1838, MANM r. 24, fr. 1243–44; unsigned letter describing campaigns, Jan 21, 1835, MANM r. 19, fr. 349–51; letter of Pérez to Comandante General, Chihuahua, #67, Feb. 16, 1837, MANM r. 19, fr. 690–701.

16. Frank McNitt, *Navajo Wars: Military Campaigns, Slave Raids and Reprisals* (Albuquerque: University of New Mexico Press, 1972), pp. 77–79; "An Account of the Chimayó Rebellion, 1837" (document 3).

17. McNitt, *Navajo Wars,* 76–79; "An Account of the Chimayó Rebellion, 1837" (document 3); letter of Pablo Salazar to Governor, Feb. 14, 1837, MANM r. 23, fr. 324–27; proceedings of the Territorial Deputation concerning misery of the militia, Nov. 21, 1836, MANM r. 21, fr. 823–26.

18. Communications sent by the Comandante Militar, New Mexico, to Comandante General, Chihuahua, Oct. 12, 1835, to Feb. 16, 1837, MANM r. 19, fr. 646–701; "An Account of the Chimayó Rebellion, 1837" (document 3).

19. "An Account of the Chimayó Rebellion, 1837" (document 3); Donaciano Vigil's address to the Departmental Assembly of New Mexico, June 22, 1846 (document 2). As his signature shows (for instance, in MANM r. 23, fr. 574), Albino Pérez spelled his first name with a "b," but since "b" and "v" were interchangeable in New Mexican Spanish, others often spelled the name "Alvino."

20. Donaciano Vigil's address, June 22, 1846 (document 2); minutes of the Departmental Assembly meeting, July 15, 1837,

MANM r. 23, fr. 740–44; letter of Juan Estevan Pino to Juan Rafael Ortiz, March 30, 1836, MANM r. 22, fr. 871; subcomisario accounts, April 1, 1836, MANM r. 22, fr. 828–1199; Secretaría de Hacienda to subcomisario of New Mexico, July 15, 1837, MANM r. 24, fr. 388; Manuel Armijo to Governor Pérez, April 12, 1837, MANM r. 23, fr. 341–42. For Sarracino's venality see "An Account of the Chimayó Rebellion, 1837" (document 3) and Herbert E. Bolton, *Guide to Materials for the History of the United States in the Principal Archives of Mexico* (Washington, D.C.: Carnegie Institute, 1913), p. 176.

21. Donaciano Vigil's address, June 22, 1846 (document 2); certificate of Juan Rafael Ortiz, Treasurer of New Mexico (October, 1837[?]) stating that the reason Doña Concepción's hundred pesos failed to arrive in the National Treasury was Apache interception of every mail leaving New Mexico (MANM r. 24, fr. 644) and see note 22 below for more on Doña Concepción; for Pérez's connection with Trinidad Trujillo, see Philip Reno, "Rebellion in New Mexico—1837," *New Mexico Historical Review* 11 (July 1965), p. 212, and Fray Angélico Chávez, "New Names in New Mexico," *El Palacio*, 64:370. Trinidad Trujillo's son Demetrio Pérez served as territorial auditor in the 1860s. He told Benjamin Read that he had come to New Mexico with his father in 1835 at the age of ten and remembered hearing his father's inaugural address (Read, *History of New Mexico* (Santa Fe, 1912), pp. 369, 603). In his memoirs, Demetrio Pérez corrected this obvious error, saying that he was seven when Mariano Martínez became governor, in 1844. Governor Martínez befriended Trinidad Trujillo when she worked as his wife's laundress, and he sent her son Demetrio to a good school (Demetrio Pérez, "Relación," June 22, 1913, Benjamin M. Read Papers, State Records Center and Archives, Santa Fe). For New Mexican views on adultery, see Janet Lecompte, "The Independent Women of Republican New Mexico, 1821–1846," *Western Historical Quarterly*, 12 (January 1981), pp. 31–32.

22. Auction of the belongings of Governor Pérez, March 3, 1838, MANM r. 25, fr. 37–39; "Account of the Effects of Albino Pérez by Concepción Alarid de Pérez, Mexico, July 11, 1838,"

MANM r. 25, fr. 68–70. Doña Concepción, who received what was left of Pérez's effects through the Santa Fe trader Jesse Sutton, wrote that some of her husband's possessions had been seized by Governor Armijo, including a "very special" new camp chair, a rifle, a red pinto horse and a mule, and Pérez's epaulets, uniform, cocked hat, and a good sword. Doña Concepción's claim that Armijo "seized" the goods is challenged in "True Account of the Effects Belonging to Señor Colonel Don Albino Pérez," (document 1). Although the "true account" in the New Mexico Archives is an unsigned and unofficial copy, it gives a detailed picture of Pérez's extravagances and debts.

23. David J. Weber, *The Taos Trappers: The Fur Trade in the Far Southwest, 1540–1846* (Norman: University of Oklahoma Press, 1968), pp. 156–90.

24. The "Memorial" of American merchants quoted in Read, *Illustrated History,* pp. 389–93, sheds light on the loans of Americans, as does "An Account of the Chimayó Rebellion, 1837: (document 3).

25. "An Account of the Chimayó Rebellion, 1837" (document 3). Municipal taxes to which the author of the "Account" refers were imposed in Santa Fe on June 9, 1836, on the stores of foreign merchants, various entertainments, and licenses (Read, *Illustrated History,* pp. 373–74n).

26. Donaciano Vigil's address, June 22, 1846 (document 2).

27. Legajo 173, Gobernación, Archivo General de la Nación (México; hereinafter cited as AGN), Mexico, re 1837 rebellion; reference through the kindness of Daniel Tyler.

28. Donaciano Vigil's address, June 22, 1846 (document 2).

29. Governor of New Mexico to Guerra y Marina, July 14, 1833, MANM r. 14, fr. 680; Donaciano Vigil's address, June 22, 1846 (document 2); Constitutional Law of Dec. 29, 1836, Manuel Dublán y José María Lozano, *Legislación mexicana o colección completa de las disposiciones legislativas expedidas desde la independencia de la república,* vol. 3 (México, 1876), pp. 230–58; George Lockhart Rives, *The United States and Mexico, 1821–1848* (New York: Charles Scribner;s Sons, 1913), vol. 1, p. 435; David J. Weber,

The Mexican Frontier, 1821–1846 (Albuquerque: University of New Mexico Press, 1982), pp. 31–35, 260–61.

30. The decrees exempting New Mexicans from paying taxes dated back to colonial days—see letter of Nemesio Salcedo, Jan. 6, 1804, in Spanish Archives of New Mexico, microfilm edition in the New Mexico State Records Center and Archives, Santa Fe, r. 15, fr. 168–69. The law of April 27, 1838, article 38, extends the exemption (Dublán y Lozano, Legislación mexicana, vol. 4, p. 494). For the law of April 17, 1837, see Dublán y Lozano, vol 3, pp. 231, 363–76; letters received from Hacienda with acknowledgment of Governor Pérez, July 8, 1837, MANM r. 23, fr. 567; and letter of Governor Pérez to Subcomisario Ambrosio Armijo, July 10, 1837, MANM r. 23, fr. 616.

31. "An Account of the Chimayó Rebellion, 1837" (document 3).

32. "An Account of the Chimayó Rebellion, 1837"; W. H. H. Davis, El Gringo, or, New Mexico and Her People (New York: Harper and Brothers, 1857), p. 87; letter of Manuel Armijo, Oct. 11, 1837 (document 8).

33. Governor's letterbook of communications sent within New Mexico, Dec. 19, 1836, to Feb. 27, 1837, MANM r. 21, fr. 748–70; letters received by the governor from Trinidad Barceló, dated March 12 and March 17, 1837, MANM r. 23, fr. 328–32; "An Account of the Chimayó Rebellion, 1837: (document 3).

34. "An Account of the Chimayó Rebellion, 1837" (document 3). In 1903 Pedro Sánchez, early biographer of Padre Antonio José Martínez, wrote a description of this incident, but it is full of errors (Sánchez, Memories of Antonio José Martínez ([Santa Fe], 1978), pp. 27–28.

35. MANM r. 24, fr. 807.

36. "An Account of the Chimayó Rebellion, 1837" (document 3).

37. Letter of Presbítero D. Fernando Ortiz to Obispo Don José Antonio de Zubiría, Santa Cruz de la Cañada, Oct. 8, 1837, AGN, Justicia, tomo 138, legajo 48 (1831–1841), 162–63. Copy in Bancroft Library, Berkeley, Cal.

38. Pérez to Ronquillo, Aug. 2, 1837, MANM r. 23, fr. 625–28.

39. *Illustrated History*, p. 375.

40. "An Account of the Chimayó Rebellion, 1837" (document 3); testimony of Juan García (document 5).

41. "An Account of the Chimayó Rebellion, 1837" (document 3). The troop had four cannon but only two were mounted, for lack of artisans to build carriages for them (Comandante Principal of New Mexico to Comandante General of Chihuahua, #63, Nov. 1, 1836, MANM r. 19, fr. 683–85). The list of men in Pérez's party is assembled from the statements of merchants taken at El Paso del Norte on Aug. 28, 1837 (document 5), Benjamin Read, *Illustrated History*, p. 390, and testimony of Francisco Sarracino, Jan. 4, 1838, in the investigation of the conduct of Sergeant Donaciano Vigil, (MANM r. 25, fr. 518–20.)

42. For description of the "road to Santa Cruz," see Adams and Chávez, eds., *The Missions of New Mexico, 1776*, pp. 46, 51, 60, 64, 72; Ralph Emerson Twitchell, *Old Santa Fe* (Danville, Ill., 1925, reprinted by Rio Grande Press, Chicago, 1963), pp. 84, 92, 137. Testimony given Jan. 4, 1838, in the investigation of the conduct of Sergeant Donaciano Vigil, establishes that the party spent the night at Pojoaque and that the battle was at La Mesilla (MANM r. 25, fr. 510–20).

43. Testimony of Francisco Sarracino, Ramón Baca, and Felipe Sena, Jan. 4, 1838, in the investigation of the conduct of Sergeant Donaciano Vigil, MANM r. 25, fr. 507–21; Donaciano Vigil, "A Statement Concerning Historical Events between 1801–1851," translated by Samuel Ellison, Ritch Collection, Huntington Library.

44. Testimony of Francisco Sarracino, Jan. 4, 1838.

45. MANM r. 25, fr. 507–21.

46. "Memoirs of Major Rafael Chacón." MS in Historical Collections, Norlin Library, University of Colorado, Boulder. Rafael Chacón was the son of Albino Chacón, who was probably the author of "An Account of the Chimayó Rebellion, 1837" (document 3).

47. "Memoirs of Major Rafael Chacón"; "An Account of the Chimayó Rebellion, 1837" (document 3).

48. Albino Chacón's "unofficial report" to the secretary of war in "Memoirs of Major Rafael Chacón"; Rafael Chacón's narrative says Pérez fought to the death with his pistols, but "True Account of the Effects Belonging to Señor Colonel Don Albino Pérez" (document 1) describes the governor's "exquisite" small rifle found in his hand when he died. For other accounts of atrocities, see "An Account of the Chimayó Rebellion, 1837" (document 3); testimony of Miranda and Gregg (document 5); letter of Manuel Armijo, Sept. 12, 1837 (document 4); and Gregg, *Commerce of the Prairies*, p. 95.

49. Davis, *El Gringo*, pp. 89–90.

50. Those killed were Pérez; the three Abréus (Ramón, Santiago, and Marcelino); Jesús María Alarid; Pablo Sáenz; Miguel Sena; Lieutenant José Hutado; Alféreces Diego Sáenz, Juan Bustamante, and Juan López; Corporal Manuel Maldonado, Clarín Guadalupe Rodríguez; the militia soldiers Jaramillo, Ortega, José Loreto Escobar, and Manuel Madrid. Francisco Sarracino and the two alcaldes of Santa Fe, Agustín Durán and Felipe Sena, were wounded, Sergeant Antonio Sena was reported killed, in error (testimony of Juan García and Guadalupe Miranda, El Paso, Aug. 28, 1837) (document 5), testimony of Francisco Sarracino, Jan. 4, 1838, MANM r. 25, fr. 515–16, Davis, *El Gringo*, pp. 89–90, "Memories of Major Rafael Chacón," "An Account of the Chimayó Rebellion, 1837" (document 3), letter of Manuel Armijo, Oct. 11, 1837 (document 8). A confused and useless account is that of Benjamin Davis Wilson, dictated to H. H. Bancroft in 1872, Bancroft Collection, Bancroft Library. For Aponte see "Account of the Services of Lieutenant Colonel Don José de Aponte," MANM r. 25, fr. 765.

51. Davis, *El Gringo*, p. 90; Gregg, *Commerce of the Prairies*, p. 94; "An Account of the Chimayó Rebellion, 1837" (document 3).

52. Letter of Carl Blumner, Santa Fe, March 18, 1841, translated by Rudolf Schroeder, Blumner papers, Library, Museum of

New Mexico (I am indebted to Carrie Arnold for the Blumner references); testimony of Josiah Gregg, El Paso del Norte, August 28, 1837 (document 5); Letter from Santa Fe, August 12, 1837 (document 6); "An Account of the Chimayó Rebellion, 1837" (document 3).

53. Albino Chacón's "unofficial report" in "Memoirs of Major Rafael Chacón"; "An Account of the Chimayó Rebellion, 1837" (document 3); Rafael García was a member of a committee on Indian affairs on March 24, 1835 (MANM r. 19, fr. 527–28), a commissioner to consider credentials of La Cañada ayuntamiento members on April 23, 1837 (MANM r. 23, fr. 867–69), and a captain in the militia of the Río Arriba district on June 5, 1846 (MANM r. 41, fr. 201).

54. Davis, *El Gringo*, p. 90; L. Bradford Prince, *Historical Sketches of New Mexico from the Earliest Records* (New York, Kansas City: Ramsey, Millett and Hudson, 1883), p. 287; Twitchell, *The Leading Facts of New Mexico History*, vol. 2, p. 63; Warren A. Beck, *New Mexico: A History of Four Centuries* (Norman: University of Oklahoma Press, 1962), p. 122. Fray Angélico Chávez, whose familiarity with New Mexico church records is unmatched, wrote in 1955 that the governor was a genízaro named José Ángel Gonzales. Chavez based this statement on a story in Pedro Sánchez's 1903 biography of Padre Antonio José Martínez, in which Governor Armijo addresses Gonzales, just before his execution, as "angelito" (little angel) and "genízaro." Pedro Sánchez is not a reliable source; Fray Angelico himself writes that Sánchez's statements must be "taken with a grain of salt." Nevertheless, Fray Angélico searched the church records for an *ángel* and a *genízaro* and located one José Ángel Gonzales, a man of mixed Taos Indian, Plains Indian, and Hispanic parentage. But there is a problem with José Ángel Gonzales—Fray Angélico's research shows that he died eight months after Governor Gonzales was supposedly executed. Fray Angélico suggests that José Ángel escaped during the battle of Pojoaque, or was reprieved from execution by Armijo, but no sources support this and many describe his death by firing squad on January 27, 1838. Fray Angélico Chávez, "José Gonzales,

Genízaro Governor," *New Mexico Historical Review* 30 (July 1955), pp. 190–94; Chávez, *But Time and Chance: The Story of Padre Martínez of Taos, 1793–1867* (Santa Fe: Sunstone Press, 1981), pp. 54–59. Note that Guadalupe Miranda, in his testimony in August, 1837 (document 5), called him "José María Gonzales."

55. "Memoirs of Major Rafael Chacón."

56. "Reporting a Junta Concerning Defense," January 1, 1834, MANM r. 18, fr. 181–89. José Gonzales's enlistment for the fall campaign of 1836 was not from Taos but from Santa Cruz— Antonio Abad Montoya headed the Santa Cruz list (MANM r. 22, fr. 814). Pérez cited Gonzales's outstanding service in a letter to the Comandante General of Chihuahua Feb. 16, 1837 (MANM r. 19, fr. 701). Fray Angélico says Gonzales was "a Taos fellow who had been residing in Santa Cruz" when he was chosen to lead the rebel forces (*But Time and Chance*, p. 54).

57. Testimony of Juan García, Guadalupe Miranda, and Josias Gregg, Aug. 28, 1837 (document 5).

58. Letter from Santa Fe, Aug. 12, 1837 in the St. Louis *Republican*, Oct. 2, 1837 (document 6).

59. MANM r. 23, fr. 631.

60. Testimony of Josias Gregg (document 5); Gregg, *Commerce of the Prairies*, p. 94; "An Account of the Chimayó Rebellion, 1837", (document 3); Davis, *El Gringo*, p. 90.

61. Letter of Antonio José Martínez to Bishop Zubiría, Sept. 25, 1837 (document 7); Hacienda records, Sept. 1, 1837, MANM r. 24, fr. 724–26.

62. Testimony of Guadalupe Miranda (document 5); letter of Manuel Armijo, Sept. 12, 1837 (document 4).

63. José Gonzales to the alcalde of Santa Clara, Aug. 11, 1837, MANM r. 23, fr. 654; Gonzales to Francisco Ortiz y Delgado, Aug. 31, 1837, Ritch Collection, Huntington Library; Francisco Ignacio de Madariaga to José Gonzales, Aug. 24, 1837, MANM r. 23, fr. 419–20; Antonio José Martínez Te Deum at Santa Cruz is mentioned in his poem of Feb. 22, 1838, in Julian Josue Vigil, "New Mexico's First Native Poet, A. J. Martínez," *Journal* (New Mexico Highlands University) 3 (Oct. 1981), p. 73. Fray Angélico

Chávez (*But Time and Chance*, p. 35–37), describes Padre Martínez's connection with the Penitentes, and Harvey Fergusson, *Rio Grande* (New York: Alfred A. Knopf, 1940), p. 192, has Padre Martínez, Manuel Armijo, and the Penitentes plotting together to develop the revolution.

64. Madariaga praised Gonzales's reasonable purposes (see note 63 above); for Ronquillo's actions, see notes 51 and 79; for sympathizers in Río Abajo, see testimony of Josias Gregg (document 5).

65. The petition in the Alvarez Papers, New Mexico State Records Center and Archives, Santa Fe, is signed by "Álvarez & Co., S. G. & H., P. M. Thompson, L. L. Waldo, Isidoro Robidoux, & others," and published in Read, *Illustrated History*, pp. 389–93. Much property escaped Governor Gonzales's generosity, as shown in the inventories of Abréu's and Pérez's property in the Ritch Collection, cited by Philip Reno, "Rebellion in New Mexico—1837," p. 203, and in the settlement of the estate of Albino Pérez, in MANM r. 25, fr. 34–70. Reno's article was one of the first to use a few of the New Mexico archives to understand the rebel side of the rebellion, but he erred in his translations. Reno mistranslated a letter of Governor Armijo dated January 25, 1838, asking for a piece of cloth from the estate of Governor Pérez to divide among the soldiers of the garrison. Reno's translation says, "Send me a list of what you have in storage of the belongings of Governor Pérez, to divide among the soldiers," indicating incorrectly that Armijo was preparing to divide up all of Pérez's goods. Reno was also mistaken in assuming that Armijo denied Pérez's widow her rightful inheritance, because evidence shows that she was not his widow (see note 21 above).

66. Minutes of the junta popular, Santa Fe, Aug. 27–29, 1837, Ritch Collection, Huntington Library, translation by Janet Lecompte.

67. Minutes of the junta popular. On the first day of the junta, Esquibel signed a letter at La Cañada, which suggests that he was not present at the meeting, or at least the early part of it (Juan Bijil, commandante de armas, and alcalde José Esquibel to the governor of Cochití, La Cañada, Aug. 27, 1837, MANM r. 23,

fr. 919–20); for Martínez's presence at the meeting, see "A Disastrous *Junta Popular,*" above.

68. Minutes of the junta popular. In 1882 or 1883, New Mexico Territorial Librarian Samuel Ellis translated the rough minutes and pieced them together to make a smooth narrative, into which he incorporated the stricken parts as though accepted by the assembly. He thus misled Philip Reno ("Rebellion in New Mexico, 1837") and others into stating that the outcome of the meeting was that Martínez, Armijo, and Esquibel were named commissioners (RI-161, Ritch Collection, Hungtington Library). If there ever was a final draft of these minutes, it has disappeared from the records; possibly the official, signed minutes would have differed from these rough notes and confirmed the assertions of the American merchants. It is barely possible that Donaciano Vigil slipped the minutes into the records later for his own reasons, as he did with other documents in later years. But it is more likely that the merchants exaggerated, as they frequently did in their dealings with New Mexico authorities.

69. "Draft of Proceedings of a Meeting of Sept. 2, 1837," MANM r. 23, fr. 637–40; for political background see "The Departmental Plan," above, or David J. Weber, *The Mexican Frontier, 1821–1846*, chapter 2.

70. J. C. [José Caballero], proclamation to alcaldes of Río Abajo, Santa Fe, Sept. 9, 1837, MANM r. 23, fr. 661–64.

71. "Draft of Proceedings of a Meeting of Sept. 2, 1837," MANM r. 23, fr. 637–40.

72. Martínez was in Taos; see his letter of Sept. 25, 1837 (document 7); for Sánchez Vergara, see "Rebels Challenged."

73. "An Account of the Chimayó Rebellion, 1837" (document 3); José Caballero's proclamation, Sept. 9, 1837.

74. Letter of Antonio José Martínez to Bishop Antonio de Zubiría, Sept. 25, 1837 (document 7); letter of Padre Juan de Jesús Trujillo to Bishop Zubiría, Albuquerque, no date, AGN, Justicia, tomo 138, legajo 48 (1831–1841), 166–68, copy in Bancroft Library. Fray Angélico Chávez cites Santiago Váldez in writ-

ing that Padre Martínez's brother José María was sent by the rebels to invite the curate to return to Taos (*But Time and Chance*, p. 56.)

75. For José Francisco Ortiz as governor, see J. María Ronquillo, Adjutant Inspector, to Captain José Caballero, Santa Fe, Sept. 5, 1837, MANM r. 23, fr. 426–27; Gefe Político to Commandante Principal, Taos, Sept. 8, 1837, MANM r. 23, fr. 658–59. The letter was written in Donaciano Vigil's hand.

76. Letter of Antonio José Martínez, Sept. 25, 1837 (document 7).

77. José Caballero's proclamation, Sept. 9, 1837.

78. "An Account of the Chimayó Rebellion, 1837" (document 3); J. María Ronquillo to José Caballero, Sept. 5, 1837, MANM r. 23, fr. 426–27; statement of military junta, Sept. 6, 1837, MANM r. 23, fr. 641–43.

79. Manuel Armijo to Guerra y Marina, Oct. 11, 1837 (document 8); subcomisario [Francisco Baca y Terrus] to José Caballero, Sept. 7, 1837, MANM r. 23, fr. 657.

80. José Hernández, "List of Gentlemen Who Have Voluntarily Provided Help for the Troop," Sept. 8, 1837, MANM r. 24, fr. 89; Manuel Armijo to Guerra y Marina, Oct. 11, 1837 (document 8); José Caballero's proclamation, Sept. 9, 1837. W. H. H. Allison writes, "Santa Fe as it Appeared during the Winter of the Years 1837 and 1838 . . .," *Old Santa Fe*, vol. 2 (Oct. 1914), p. 174, that Vicente Sánchez Vergara was a lawyer from Mexico. He is in error: Sánchez Vergara was a native New Mexican, baptized at Laguna, N.M., March 4, 1807; Fray Angélico Chávez, *Origins of New Mexico Families in the Spanish Colonial Period* (Santa Fe: Historical Society of New Mexico, 1954), p. 282. He served in various governmental positions until he became deputy from New Mexico to the national congress, from 1838 until 1845.

81. José Caballero's proclamation, Sept. 9, 1837.

82. Letter of Manuel Armijo, Oct. 11, 1837 (document 8).

83. W. H. H. Allison, "Santa Fe as it Appeared during the Winter of the Years 1837 and 1838 . . .," pp. 170–72; Allison, "Colonel Francisco Perea," *Old Santa Fe*, 1 (Oct. 1913) p. 211.

84. Manuel Armijo's service record, Oct. 19, 1841, Lilly Library, University of Indiana, Bloomington. I am indebted to Dr. Will Wroth for calling my attention to these documents.

85. Plan of Tomé, published in *Diario del Gobierno*, Oct. 19, 1837.

86. Plan of Tomé, and "An Account of the Chimayó Rebellion, 1837" (document 3).

87. Letter of Manuel Armijo to Guerra y Marina, Sept. 12, 1837 (document 4).

88. "An Account of the Chimayó Rebellion, 1837" (document 3); certificate of Francisco Ortiz y Delgado, first alcalde of Santa Fe, Sept. 13, 1837, MANM r. 23, fr. 902, and of Felipe Sena, second alcalde of Santa Fe, same date, MANM r. 23, fr. 903. These certificates are copies; the signatures of the alcaldes and witnesses are not original, but the rubric of José Gonzales appears to be, for it corresponds to another document written in Vicente Sánchez Vergara's hand and "signed" by José Gonzales (MANM r. 23, fr. 654).

89. Manuel Armijo's letter of Oct. 11, 1837 (document 8); "An Account of the Chimayó Rebellion, 1837" (document 3).

90. Allison, "Santa Fe as it Appeared during the Winter of the Year 1837 and 1838," p. 172; "Acceptance of Armijo as Chief of the Liberating Army by the Military," MANM r. 23, fr. 644–45, signed by Armijo and Mariano Chávez from the Río Abajo army, and the presidial officers José Caballero, José Silva, José Hernández, Esquipulas Caballero, Francisco Martínez, Manuel Ramírez, Rafael Tapia, Baltazar Sandoval, José de Larrañaga, and Antonio Sena.

91. Letter of Manuel Armijo, Oct. 11, 1837 (document 8); "An Account of the Chimayó Rebellion, 1837" (document 8); Armijo to the first alcalde of Santa Fe, Sept. 18, 1837, MANM r. 23, fr. 665–66; Armijo to the foreign merchants, Sept. 24, 1837, MANM r. 23, fr. 670–71; treasury records, MANM r. 24, fr. 668–69 and r. 25, fr. 1259–62.

92. Juan Estevan Pino to Armijo, Sept. 19, 1837, MANM r. 23, fr. 446; Armijo to Minister of War, May 1, 1840, "Official Mexican Correspondence and Documents, Capture and Disposi-

tion of Prisoners of Texas Expedition to Santa Fe," frac. 1, leg. 1, Operaciones Militares (1841–42), Archivo de Guerra, Bolton Transcripts, Bancroft Library; Armijo to Minister of War #20, Jan. 2, 1842, MANM r. 28, fr. 1476–77; Minister of War to Armijo, Oct. 16, 1843, Secretaría de la Defensa Nacional, XI/481. 3/1714, frac. 1 [no legajo number] Operaciones Militares (1841–44). Twice Armijo retreated in the face of battle—in 1843, before the Snively forces, and in 1846, before the American invasion; Daniel Tyler, "Governor Armijo's Moment of Truth," *Journal of the West,* 11 (April 1972), pp. 307–16, and Lecompte, "Manuel Armijo and the Americans," *Journal of the West* 14 (July 1980), pp. 57, 60.

93. Circular of acting governor Donaciano Vigil to the people, Santa Fe, Jan. 22, 1847, U.S. Congress, House Executive Document 70, 30th Cong., 1st Sess. (Ser. 521), p. 21; report of Colonel Sterling Price, Santa Fe, Feb. 15, 1847, *Niles National Register,* April 24, 1847, p. 121. A different Montoya was a well-known alcalde of Santa Fe and landowner, who died in 1842; Ralph Emerson Twitchell, *The Spanish Archives of New Mexico* (Cedar Rapids: Torch Press, 1914), 1:50, 169, 270.

94. Letter of Manuel Armijo, Oct. 11, 1837 (document 8). No copies of the treaty, nor of correspondence between Armijo and Pablo Montoya, nor of documents cited in the body of Armijo's report, remain in MANM or in other archives consulted. They were undoubtedly sent to Mexico and may still be in the archives there.

95. "An Account of the Chimayó Rebellion, 1837" (document 3).

96. Letter of Manuel Armijo, Oct. 11, 1837 (document 8). The rebel sentence against the archives was mercifully suspended, although some documents for 1837 may have been destroyed, since relatively few remain for that year.

97. Letter of Manuel Armijo, Oct. 11, 1837 (document 8); circular of acting governor Donaciano Vigil to the people, Santa Fe, Jan. 22, 1847. Who were the unfortunate Montoyas, Esquibel, and Chopón?

Antonio Abad Montoya and his brother Desiderio were literate men of respected family. Antonio Abad's name headed the militia list of 1836 and was dignified with *don*, as José Gonzales's name on the same list was not (MANM r. 22, fr. 814). Padre Martínez wrote that the Montoyas were nephews of the late Abán Córdoba and were related to a city councilman of Taos; they were now imprisoned in Santa Fe because they were movers of the first mob and involved in the second (document 7).

Juan José Esquibel was fifty years old in 1837 and married to Rafaela Martín; Santa Cruz census of 1823, in Virginia Lanham Olmstead, *Spanish and Mexican Censuses of New Mexico, 1750–1830* (Albuquerque: New Mexico Genealogical Society, 1981), pp. 195, 223. He was alcalde of La Cañada and a relative of the Montoyas, as Padre Martínez tells us (document 7). Esquibel founded the Cantón and signed his letters "Commander of the Cantón."

Juan Vigil signed as "Commander of arms." He was known as "el Chopón" and "General Chopón," meaning of short stature; W. H. H. Allison, "Santa Fe . . . ," *Old Santa Fe 2* (Oct. 1914), p. 174; Rubén Cobos, *A Dictionary of New Mexican and Southern Colorado Spanish* (Santa Fe: Museum of New Mexico Press, 1983), p. 49. He was called "El Chepón" (diminuitive of José[?]) in Padre Martínez's décima of Feb. 22, 1838; New Mexico Highlands University *Journal 3* (Oct. 1981), p. 73. Fray Angélico Chávez believed this to be a reference to José Gonzales and not to Juan Vigil (*But Time and Chance*, p. 54). Rafael Chacón ("Memoirs") tells of the wounding of Captain Aponte at the battle of La Mesilla by the rebel called "El Quemado," whose true name was Vigil. As Captain Aponte ran El Quemado through with a lance, the rebel shot Aponte with an arrow in the abdomen, but both men got caught in a cord and *tilma* (small blanket) that El Quemado had tied around him as armor, and fought hand to hand until they fell exhausted. Juan Vigil was probably Juan Bautista Vigil y Martín, alcalde of La Cañada in 1832, town councilman of San José de las Trampas later that year (MANM r. 14, fr. 616–19, 1054). On Sept. 28, 1837, Lieutenant Rafael Tapia visited Juan Vigil y Martín in the Santa Fe jail, to take his deposition about a letter incriminating him. Tapia suggested the letter be sent to Pablo Montoya, "as commander of that division." Armijo answered that the accusers of Vigil y Martín must produce proof of their accusation (MANM r. 23, fr. 449–52). An anonymous décima on the rebellion characterizes "El Chopón" as one of the worst of the rebels, along with Rafael García (document 12). Philip Reno ("Rebellion in New Mexico") is incorrect in stating that Juan Vigil was alcalde of San Juan Pueblo, the result of misreading the signatures of Juan Vigil and Juan José Esquibel in a letter to the governor of Cochití, Aug. 27, 1837 (MANM r. 23, fr. 920).

98. Lecompte, "Manuel Armijo and the Americans," pp. 51–53.

99. Gregg, *Commerce of the Prairies*, pp. 92–97; Kendall, *Narrative*, 1:346–61; Davis, *El Gringo*, pp. 85–97. For Davis's embezzling, see A. G. Mayers to Hon. G. W. Manypenny, Santa Fe, Feb. 28, 1856; J. L. Collins to A. G. Mayers, Santa Fe, Oct. 6, 1856; and to W. H. H. Davis, May 20, 1857, as well as other letters in Letters Received by the Office of Indian Affairs, 1824–81, New Mexico Superintendency, National Archives, Washington, D.C., Microcopy 234, roll 548.

100. Kendall, *Narrative*, 1:372–73; Gregg, *Commerce of the Prairies*, pp. 95–96; Davis, *El Gringo*, pp. 86, 91; Armijo to Pérez, April 12, 1837, MANM r. 23, fr. 341–42.

101. "A Statement of Governor Donaciano Vigil," translated by Samuel Ellison, Ritch collection (RI-80), Huntington Library.

102. José María de Arze, Comandante General of Chihuahua to Governor and Comandante Principal of New Mexico, March 6, 1838, MANM r. 24, fr. 1076–77; Vicente Sánchez Vergara, México, May 12, 1841, to Manuel Armijo, MANM r. 28, fr. 1217–22. For Governor Chico and the Californios, see Weber, *The Mexican Frontier*, pp. 255–60. For Padre Martínez, see note 63, above.

103. Armijo's proclamation to the alcaldes, Sept. 24, 1837, MANM r. 23, fr. 672–73; Read's *Illustrated History*, p. 383, has a translation of it.

104. Kendall, *Narrative* I, pp. 350–51.

105. *Commerce of the Prairies*, p. 96; Davis, *El Gringo*, p. 91.

106. No copy of Armijo's apppointment is with the New Mexico archives, but two pieces of evidence show that it existed. One is the decision of the New Mexico Departmental Assembly, in 1839, to grant Armijo an annual salary of 4,500 pesos, retroactive to Sept. 12, 1837, when "by supreme order" Armijo was appointed governor and political chief (salary accounts citing action of the assembly, April 27, 1839, MANM r. 24, fr. 691). The other is a personal letter to Armijo from General José J. Calvo, commanding general at Chihuahua, dated Sept. 30, 1837, saying that this letter is official notice to Armijo that he has been named governor and that Juan Rafael Ortiz has been named treasurer of the department. General Calvo wrote that he considered sending Armijo the appointments by extraordinario, but thought better to bring them himself, so they would not get lost (MANM r. 23, fr. 305–6). General Calvo did not bring the appointments after all, but apparently sent them with the Veracruz squadron, which arrived at Santa Fe on Jan. 9, 1838.

107. Circular of Manuel Armijo, Oct. 5, 1837.

108. Circular of Manuel Armijo, Oct. 5, 1837.

109. For Armijo's old wound, see Kendall, *Narrative*, 1:360; private letter of Armijo, MANM r. 33, fr. 606–7; proceedings of a military junta, Santa Fe, Oct. 21, 1837, MANM r. 23, fr. 649–51.

110. Letterbook of Comandante Principal, 1837, MANM r. 23, fr. 465–66.

111. Letter of Juan Estevan Pino to Armijo, Oct. 21, 1837, MANM r. 23, fr. 465–66; proceedings of a military junta, Oct. 21, 1837.

112. Proceedings of a military junta, Oct. 21, 1837.

113. Letter of Armijo to Caballero, Oct. 23, 1837, Ritch Coll. (RI-167), Huntington Library.

114. Letter of Juan Rafael Ortiz to Manuel Armijo, Santa Fe, Nov. 1, 1837, MANM r. 23, fr. 483–85.

115. Hacienda records, MANM r. 24, fr. 668–69; and r. 25,

fr. 1259–62. Armijo may have returned to Santa Fe by Nov. 24, as indicated by a document approving a request of Manuel Álvarez for land, but the document may be a forgery; Ocaté Grant Papers, Surveyor General's files, Report 143 (microfilm roll 26, frame 7, Records Center and Archives, Santa Fe).

116. Comandante General of Chihuahua to Armijo, Nov. 15, 1837, MANM r. 23, fr. 307–8; *Partes del Gral. Manuel Armijo, Gobernador y Comandante Militar de Nuevo-México, E.U.A. dando cuenta de las operaciones efectuadas con motivo del pronunciamiento de la población,* 1838, Secretaría de la Defensa Nacional, Exp. XI/481.3/1221. Lansing Bartlett Bloom, "New Mexico under Mexican Administration," *Old Santa Fe 2* (July 1914), p. 30n, writes that Captain Pedro Muñoz of the Veracruz squadron arrived early in October from El Paso del Norte in advance of the dragoons, but the archives show that Muñoz had been in Santa Fe since February 1838, and viséed the muster rolls of the Santa Fe Presidial Company through 1837 on the third day of every month excepting November (Military Records, 1838, MANM r. 24, fr. 5–70 passim, 313.

117. Letter of Armijo to ayuntamiento of Taos, Jan. 2, 1838, MANM r. 21, fr. 805–6; Lieutenant Colonel Cayetano Justiniani, "Diario de novedades . . .," Jan. 10, 1838, in *Partes del Gral. Manuel Armijo . . .*; account of troops in New Mexico, 1838, MANM r. 25, fr. 525–98. The discrepancy in numbers of troops in Justiniani's diary and Carlos María Bustamante's account (document 13) may be explained by gaps in the extant records in the archives, which fail to show that more troops arrived in Santa Fe after January 9.

118. Proclamation of Manuel Armijo. Jan. 7, 1838[?] (document 9); MANM r. 24, fr. 1311–13.

119. MANM r. 24, fr. 1311–12.

120. Read, *Illustrated History,* p. 385, translated this document very literally in order to expose it as a "literary abortion" and its author as a "consummate ignoramus"; Lansing B. Bloom, "New Mexico under Mexican Administration," *Old Santa Fe 2* (July 1914), p. 35n, gives it a much better and fairer translation.

121. Circular of Jan. 19, 1838 (document 10); letter of Manuel Armijo to Commander of the reunión at La Cañada, Jan. 22, 1838, MANM r. 24, fr. 1320–22.

122 Letter of Armijo to Comandante de Armas and secretary of the alcaldes of Ábiquiu and Ojo Caliente, Jan. 23, 1838, MANM r. 24, fr. 1323–24.

123. Circular of Manuel Armijo, Jan. 24, 1838 (document 11).

124. Santa Fe *New Mexican*, Jan. 7, 1907, p. 6, c. 4; Davis, *El Gringo*, p. 92.

125. George Lockhart Rives, *The United States and Mexico, 1821–1848*, 1:336–37. For La Garita see Bruce T. Ellis, "La Garita: Santa Fe's Little Spanish Fort," *El Palacio* 84 (summer 1978).

126. Kendall, *Narrative*, 1:350, 360.

127. "Memoirs of Major Rafael Chacón"; W. H. H. Allison, "Santa Fe . . . as Narrated by the Late Colonel Francisco Perea," *Old Santa Fe 2* (Oct. 1914), pp. 174–75. However brutal the execution appeared to young Perea, he later acknowledged its success in checking would-be revolutionists.

128. Carlos María Bustamante, *El Gabinete Mexicano* (document 13). Carlos Santistevan killed Antonio Vigil and was rewarded with fifty pesos ("Petition of Carlos Santistevan, Mar. 6, 1838," MANM r. 24, fr. 1174–75); L. Bradford Prince, *Historical Sketches of New Mexico*, p. 288, says that Juan Antonio Vigil was executed near Cuyamungué.

129. Kendall, *Narrative*, 1:350; Gregg, *Commerce of the Prairies*, pp. 96–97; "Memoirs of Major Rafael Chacón."

130. "Memoirs of Major Rafael Chacón"; Sánchez, *Memories of Antonio José Martínez*, ed. Guadalupe Baca-Vaughn n.p., 1978), pp. 30–31.

131. Prince, *Historical Sketches of New Mexico*, pp. 288–89. The death of José Gonzales by firing squad, on Jan. 27, 1838, is described by Pedro Sánchez, *Memories of Antonio José Martínez*, pp. 31–32; by Santiago Valdez, "Biografía," Ritch Coll. (RI-2211), Huntington Library; by Gregg, *Commerce of the Prairies*, p. 97; by Kendall, *Narrative*, 1:350; by Davis, *El Gringo*, p. 92; and by scores of followers in the next hundred and forty-odd years. I have located

no primary source describing the death of José Gonzales, but many of these writers were alive and in New Mexico at that time or a few years after. Sánchez and Valdez were related to Padre Martínez, who heard Gonzales's confession before his execution, according to their accounts.

132. "Apologia of Presbyter Antonio J. Martínez [1838]," *New Mexico Historical Review* 3 (Oct. 1928), pp. 340–41.

133. Davis, *El Gringo*, p. 303; letter of Santiago Martínez to Armijo, Taos, March 8, 1838, MANM r. 24, fr. 1168–70; letter of Juan Andres Archuleta, prefect of Río Arriba, to Armijo, March 10, 1838, MANM r. 24, fr. 1181–83.

134. No definitive biography of Manuel Armijo exists, but these judgments on him find some documentary basis in the following: Minge, "Frontier Problems"; Daniel Tyler, "Gringo Views of Governor Manuel Armijo," *New Mexico Historical Review* 45 (Jan. 1970); Tyler, "Governor Armijo's Moment of Truth," *Journal of the West* 11 (April 1972); Weber, *The Mexican Frontier*; and Lecompte, "Manuel Armijo and the Americans."

Index